CONTENTS

PART THREE: ENTERING INTO YOUR TRUE WORK

A 90-DAY DEVOTIONAL

SUCCESS WITH PURPOSE AND POWER

DR. MYLES MUNROE

WHITAKER HOUSE

This devotional is based on material from *The Principles and Power of Success: Charting the Path to Purpose, Excellence, and Influence* by Dr. Myles Munroe, © 2025 by Munroe Group of Companies Ltd., published by Whitaker House.

Boldface type in Scripture quotations indicates the author's emphasis.

The forms *LORD* and *GOD* (in small capital letters) in Bible quotations represent the Hebrew name for God *Yahweh* (Jehovah), while *Lord* and *God* normally represent the name *Adonai*, in accordance with the Bible version used.

SUCCESS WITH PURPOSE AND POWER:
A 90-Day Devotional

Munroe Global • P.O. Box N9583 • Nassau, Bahamas
www.munroeglobal.com
office@munroeglobal.com

ISBN: 979-8-88769-455-9 • eBook ISBN: 979-8-88769-456-6
Printed in the United States of America

Whitaker House • 1030 Hunt Valley Circle • New Kensington, PA 15068
www.whitakerhouse.com

Library of Congress Control Number: 2025943786

1 2 3 4 5 6 7 8 9 10 𝐖 31 30 29 28 27 26 25

PART FIVE: RECOGNIZING THE POWER OF INFLUENCE

INTRODUCTION

For thirty years, Dr. Myles Munroe counseled and guided multitudes of people to live a life of personal fulfillment and social and spiritual well-being. The knowledge and experience he gained led him to the conclusion that the central principle of life is *purpose*—and that our success comes from knowing our purpose and living it out.

As Dr. Munroe reveals in this devotional, "Everything in our life, including our potential for success, is related to our personal purpose. The significance of this is that following your purpose will inevitably lead to your success. No matter who you are, you have within you the power to be successful."

Accordingly, Dr. Munroe explains that success, for each one of us, is personal and individual. This is because success isn't about beating someone else at a race or dominating others. It is about accomplishing the unique, God-given purpose you were born to fulfill. "What I am presenting here can turn you into a different person," Dr. Munroe expresses. "As you learn what it means to be successful, you may be introduced to yourself for the first time."

An essential concept in Dr. Munroe's teachings is that success does not come by *doing* something but by *becoming* something. You will learn how you were innately designed to be successful so that you can identify and develop your inherent gifting. Among other vital principles, you will also discover how to activate the laws of success, employ strategies to prosper in your domain, and initiate the ten keys for personal success. Dr. Munroe emphasizes that, in order to protect the longevity of your success, you must commit to developing personal character and to identifying and establishing the values and standards by which you will conduct your life.

All these aspects will lead to your naturally exerting influence in the world. When you grow in your purpose, exercising your potential and gifting, your success will flourish, and you will make an impact on those around you, transforming your environment. Success is about serving your gift to the world and being a positive influence on others as you reflect the nature of God's kingdom on earth.

Each entry in this devotional features insights and encouragement from Dr. Munroe's transformative teachings in his book *The Principles and Power of Success,* as well as a motivating thought for the day. One of the ten keys for personal success that Dr. Munroe teaches is prayer, through which you can connect with the Source of your purpose—and, ultimately, your success. *Success with Purpose and Power* will encourage you to seek the One who loves you, planted your purpose within you, and desires to guide you to its fulfillment.

Also featured in this devotional are daily Scripture readings. Since it is the Creator, our "Manufacturer," who has given us our purpose and gifting, it is essential that we read His "Manufacturer's Manual," as Dr. Munroe liked to call the Bible, for ourselves in order to clearly see the revelation of His purposes. We must allow

God's Word to dwell richly in our heart so that, as we meditate on and absorb Scripture, it truly becomes a part of us.

Whenever we study the Manufacturer's Manual, we should also ask God for wisdom to understand and apply it. The Holy Spirit is our Teacher, and we need Him to illuminate God's Word to us and give us insight. May God bless you in your relationship with Him as you successfully fulfill your God-given purpose in your generation.

— Day 1 —

DESTINED FOR SUCCESS

"'I know the plans I have for you,' announces the Lord. *'I want you to enjoy success. I do not plan to harm you. I will give you hope for the years to come.'"*

—Jeremiah 29:11 (nirv)

Everyone wants to be successful. I've never met anyone who planned to fail. I believe that each human being on earth—regardless of race, nationality, background, and other factors—desires, and is designed for, success.

While everyone desires to succeed, the idea of success can be elusive. Let me propose to you a working definition that applies to all people, regardless of circumstances: *Success means accomplishing the purpose you were put on this earth to fulfill.*

Everything in our life, including our potential for success, is related to our personal purpose. This means that *following your purpose will inevitably lead to your success.* No matter who you are, you have within you the power to be successful.

You might already consider yourself to be a success in your chosen field, whether that is business, law, education, or something else, but you want to learn additional principles for increased success. It could be that you feel successful in one area of your life but want to know how to succeed in other areas as well. Or maybe you have never felt like a success and want to learn the foundational precepts for being successful and prosperous. The principles in this devotional apply equally to all of these areas; they are principles from which we can continually draw and grow throughout our life.

In what ways should we measure our success as we follow our personal purpose? I like to say that success is what you've done compared to what you were designed to do. We measure our success by our individual calling and abilities.

Suppose a bird that was designed to fly has never flown because it has never put forth the effort to do so. That bird has missed its purpose. Yet if the bird spreads its wings and flies because it's the bird's nature to do so, it is successful—it is doing what it was meant to do.

To succeed, you need to first discover what you were meant to do—what you're supposed to be doing—because of your inherent gifts.

Most people have not yet captured what they were born to do. If we haven't been fulfilling our purpose up to now, we may have failed to be successful—but I believe that failure is just postponed success. We can begin to fly in our gifting, no matter what our past.

Thought: Success means accomplishing the purpose you were put on this earth to fulfill.

Reading: Ephesians 2:10

—DAY 2—

IT ISN'T A COMPETITION

"In truth I perceive that God shows no partiality."
—Acts 10:34 (NKJV)

It is easy to base our success on what we are doing compared to what others are doing. Yet success is not what we've done compared to what others have done. That's called competition. We'll always find someone who seems to have achieved more than we have—or less than we have. We'll always encounter someone whose skills seem more advanced than ours—or less advanced than ours. Since each person has a personal purpose, we can't measure our success by comparing ourselves with anyone else. Success means forgetting about competing with others and focusing on pursuing our own gift, or "assignment," in this world.

One time, when I was a young student, I was very excited because I received the top mark in my class on an exam. The only problem was, my grade was a 48! That meant that everybody else received a grade of less than 48. When I showed my mother my test, she said, "You got first in the class with a 48? Forty-eight out of what?"

Even though I was at the top of my class with a grade of 48, I had failed the test because the answer to "Forty-eight out of what?" was "100." According to the criteria of the test examiner, even though I received the highest score, I didn't demonstrate that I comprehended the material; in fact, I demonstrated that I had failed to grasp it well. Students may not always receive 100 percent on all their school exams, but, in this context, success may be defined as the degree to which the student fulfilled the original assignment or purpose for which the test was administered.

By what are you evaluating your own success? Success is not about beating someone else in a race. Perhaps you have felt like you were getting by in life in comparison to others, but do you know how you are doing compared to your personal assignment or goal? And how do you determine that? In coming devotions, we'll explore how to discover and live out our true purpose and gifting.

Again, success means doing everything you can to develop what you were made to do. You don't have to worry about being successful—if you serve your gift, you will succeed!

In this devotional, I'll explain exactly what I mean by serving your gift. I teach truths and practical guidelines that I have learned over a span of forty-five years, from the time I was a teenager living in poverty and discovering my true potential. My purpose is to equip you with the knowledge and principles necessary for achieving personal success. I want to help you to achieve your goals and aspirations, and to fulfill the plan for your life.

Thought: Success is not about beating someone else in a race but discovering and fulfilling your personal purpose in life.

Reading: Romans 14:12

—Day 3—

THE TOP FIVE QUESTIONS IN LIFE

"[God] *has made everything beautiful in its time. He has also set eternity in the human heart; yet no one can fathom what God has done from beginning to end.*" —Ecclesiastes 3:11

All of human life can be reduced to five questions that motivate everything people do on this planet. Every issue that humans face is related to these questions because our attempt to find the answers to them leads to our behavior—whether that behavior is positive or negative. And for you to be successful in life, you must eventually be able to answer them for yourself.

1. *"Who am I?"* This question is a matter of *identity*. Many of us still struggle with self-identity. That is why most of us are "other people": when we have no established identity for ourselves, we may follow the lifestyles of others in order to try to imitate the way those individuals present themselves.

2. *"Where am I from?"* Most of us think of this question in geographical terms, but it is a question of *human origin*. The answer has to do with the ultimate source of our being or existence.

   If you try to find out where you are from by using your national or ethnic heritage, you will get lost. Here's the problem: you can't know who you are (question number 1) until you find out where you are from (question number 2). And you can't find out where you are from if you don't know who you are. The two questions are interconnected.

3. *"Why am I here?"* This is perhaps the most difficult question most people battle with, and it is directly tied to the

issue of *purpose*. It's also tied to questions 1 and 2. If you don't know where you are from and don't know who you are, you'll never know why you are here.

4. *"What am I able to do?"* This question might be phrased, "What am I capable of?" It is a matter of *potential*. Potential indicates, "What is my true ability in life?" or "What is my true power in the world?" I believe that a majority of people are living below their ability. The problem is that our society often attempts to tell us what we can and cannot do.
5. *"Where am I going?"* This is a question of destiny. What am I aiming for, and how will I know when I arrive? Where am I headed, now and in the future? We'll cover this question, also, as we progress through this devotional because the combined answers to these questions form the foundation or framework for success in all areas of life.

Thought: You must answer each of life's top five questions for yourself if you are to discover your purpose and be successful.

Reading: Psalm 36:5–9

— Day 4 —

PURSUING YOUR PURPOSE

"It is God who is at work in you, both to desire and to work for His good pleasure." —Philippians 2:13 (NASB)

Success is not a pursuit; it is the *result* of fulfilling your purpose in life—coming to know who you are, where you're from, why you're here, what you can do, and where you're going. But although success is not something we pursue, it is still a journey that we will follow for our entire life because our purpose is a lifelong gift. We can't be laid off or fired from our purpose, and our gifting doesn't have a retirement clause. You will have success in increments throughout your life on your way to fulfilling your ultimate purpose.

Thus, success has more to do with moving in the right direction than coming to a destination. It really is a process rather than an end. When you consider your success to be based on the process you undergo to fulfill your ultimate purpose, then you are a success!

How many people are going through life looking shiny and beautiful but not fulfilling their true purpose? Purpose determines success, so if someone wears expensive clothing but doesn't do what they were born to do, they are simply a well-dressed failure. Or if someone rides around in a new car with all the amenities but isn't exercising their true gifts, they are merely a well-equipped failure. Life is not about how expensive our clothes and car are. What's important is whether we are doing what we were created to do. In this way, we can truly live and become prosperous while blessing the world with our contributions. And we discover what we were made to do by recognizing our inherent gifting.

Everyone has one or perhaps two main gifts. To have a successful life in which we are fulfilling the purpose for which we were born, we must discover our primary gifting and learn to deploy it. As we do, we can encourage ourselves with these principles:

- *The gift you were born with is more important than the skills you have.* We are not born with skills—we have to learn them. So, there's something higher than skills, which is our inherent gift.
- *You can never lose what you were born with.* Your gift is always with you. It will outlast your skills and keep moving you along in your life's journey.
- *Your future is not ahead of you; it's inside you.* Because you were born with a gift, or a "seed," the key to your life is to discover, develop, and serve this seed-gift to the world. The gift is there—you just need look for it within you.

Thought: Your gift is inside you, waiting to be discovered and developed.

Reading: 2 Corinthians 9:8

—DAY 5—

DISCOVERING YOUR GIFT

"Before I formed you in the womb I knew you; before you were born I sanctified you; I ordained you a prophet to the nations." —Jeremiah 1:5 (NKJV)

How do you know what you were born to do? You can begin by answering the following vital questions. After answering them, think about your answers and notice recurring themes and patterns. When you do, you will have identified your primary gift.

1. *"What is my greatest desire?"* What do you envision yourself doing? What do you hope to accomplish in life? What would you like more than anything else?
2. *"What do I wish for humanity?"* Have you ever asked, "Why doesn't somebody do ____________?" or, "I wish somebody would invent ____________"? Whatever you complain about, you may be born to help fix!
3. *"What is my deepest passion?"* When you are passionate about doing something, you want to be involved in it and keep doing it. That is a good indication of what your gift is.
4. *"What are my natural abilities?"* What obvious talents and abilities do you exhibit? What are you good at and truly enjoy engaging in? What have others told you that you are gifted at doing?
5. *"What do I think about being or doing when I am by myself?"* Many people in history heard the call of their gift when they were alone. Set aside time to be alone and listen to your heart.

6. *"What would I do even if I weren't paid for it?"* What you were born to do is something that you would do and be happy doing even if you weren't paid for it. People who are effective and change the world never do anything for money alone. They do it because they love it and are passionate about it.
7. *"What would I do even if it meant personal sacrifice?"* For example, when people find their gift, they're normally willing to sacrifice financially to invest in the idea or in making the idea a reality.
8. *"What makes me angry?"* Whatever makes you angry is a sign of what you were born to do or to help change. Many successful people were motivated by anger or indignation about injustice or unmet needs in society. To find your gift, look for what stirs you inside.
9. *"What do I wish I could change in/about my country?"* It may be that your passion and gifts will lead you to pursue reforms and improvements in your own community and/or nation.
10. *"What would I do if I had limitless money and resources with which to do it?"* What endeavor would you pursue if you had all the money you could want? Your answer to that question is what you were born to do.

There is an ancient proverb that makes a powerful statement in regard to our gifting: *"A man's gift makes room for him"* (Proverbs 18:16 NKJV). You were designed to be known for your gift. That is where your success lies. You have to consider, "What is my gift? What is my assignment? What is my reason for being here?"

Thought: Your passions will point to your purpose.

Reading: 1 Corinthians 10:31

—Day 6—

TRUE SUCCESS

"You will know the truth, and the truth will set you free."
—John 8:32

I hope you will enjoy exploring the ten questions I shared in yesterday's devotion. You may have to dig deep to find some of the answers, but the work will be worth it. I want you to discover your true gift in life. I care about you, and I want you to be a success. I don't want you to fail. I know life can be rough, and I want you to understand the principles of success and to develop the inner reserves to meet life's challenges.

You may have been waiting a long time for success and prosperity. You don't have to be a beggar. You're a great person with much more inside you that no one has yet seen. You are not finished. You're still on your way. So, wake up and dust yourself off. Find your gift and pursue it! You will become free from the lies people have told you about yourself—or the lies you've told yourself—about who you are and what you can do.

If you have been on a vocational track that has been financially profitable but ultimately makes you feel empty inside, or you want to do something else that is truly meaningful to you, I want you to know the truth about yourself because the truth that you know will set you free. (See John 8:32.)

People often need to work through a sequence of thoughts, emotions, and conclusions before they make a decision to take action. They may initially be resistant to doing something, but as they identify the reasons for their lack of action—perhaps a need for more knowledge or skills—they can begin to take steps toward making their dream a reality.

Until you find your true calling, you will never be satisfied. Your purpose is the only thing that is right for you. You may be familiar with the saying, "The enemy of right is not wrong. The enemy of right is 'good.'" You may think your life is going along fine because you're doing something good—but are you doing the right thing? Are you using your gift to fulfill your unique purpose? We can't allow ourselves to be distracted by good things. If we are doing something good, we may have a job or be contributing on some level, but we have not yet found our true gift.

When you find your purpose and fulfill it, that's success.

Thought: True success consists in finding your purpose and fulfilling it.

Reading: Psalm 37:4

—Day 7—

LIFE'S LAWS MAKE SUCCESS PREDICTABLE

"'This is the covenant I will make with the people of Israel after that time,' declares the Lord. 'I will put my law in their minds and write it on their hearts.'" —Jeremiah 31:33

Recognizing our inherent gift is a powerful first step, but we also need to understand how to activate it by employing life's laws of success. Unless we follow these laws, we will not fulfill our true purpose. Everything exists by laws and according to laws. Laws are the glue that holds the universe together.

Let me make what might seem like a bold statement: Success is *predictable*—and so is failure.

I can make that statement because, as I wrote above, everything in life was meant to function according to laws, and our response to those laws—positive or negative—makes all of life predictable. You can predict whether a person will succeed or fail because of the way life is designed. By "designed," I'm not referring to the systems of a particular culture or society, and I'm not talking about ritual laws. I'm talking about the laws that are built into life.

Therefore, the way you relate to life depends on the laws that you know and put into practice. Learning and following these laws is the secret to success and prosperity.

People spend millions of dollars going to all sorts of seminars and reading all kinds of positive-thinking and how-to-succeed books, and they are still broke and lacking purpose because they don't understand that you can't succeed by using another person's ideas. You need your own revelation of those ideas. They have to become yours. In the same way, I cannot believe the laws of success for you. I can only encourage you to make them your own and to act on them.

Unless we have a good grasp of life's laws of success, we won't comprehend their importance, and we won't exercise them properly. In the next several devotions, I lay the groundwork for you to understand the purpose and meaning of these laws—their nature and how they function—so that you can effectively put them into practice. We will begin by looking at the principles that clarify, step-by-step, the ideas about laws I have just described for you so that they can be established as a foundation for success in your life.

Thought: Success is predictable when you understand and practice the laws of life.

Reading: Jeremiah 29:13

—Day 8—

KEY PRINCIPLES OF SUCCESS, PART 1

"The law of the Lord *is perfect, refreshing the soul. The statutes of the* Lord *are trustworthy, making wise the simple."* —Psalm 19:7

I established on day 1 of this devotional that every human being on earth has been designed for success. This is a principle that holds true for all of creation: everything in life was designed to succeed. I didn't always understand this principle because, having been born into a low-income environment, I was taught that merely surviving was enough. As a result, I developed a survival mentality. A survival mentality will always be a poverty mentality because this mindset keeps you from believing that you deserve to prosper. You can actually become afraid of success.

Many people are poor because they are afraid to be wealthy. They are mentally convinced that they don't deserve to prosper. They're actually afraid of what they want, and so they reject it rather than pursuing and accepting it. Whatever you are afraid of stays away from you. To get past this mentality, I had to discover the inherent law that everything in creation was designed to succeed.

That was a paradigm shift for me because it meant rejecting the mindset of my upbringing and the low expectations of society regarding what I could be. I even had to be convinced that every human being *wants* to be successful. You must recognize that the desire or hunger in your heart to be a success is natural.

Now, that makes life very tough for many people, doesn't it? It is the very source of their depression. Their desire for success discourages them because they know what they want to be, but they don't know how to get there. So, although they hate where they are, they feel stuck. The first step toward addressing your hunger for success is to affirm that you were designed to succeed. Success will not come about until your thinking changes. Therefore, you must believe that everyone—yourself included—is designed to succeed.

Along the same lines, it is because everything was designed to succeed that everything on earth also has laws attached to it—laws that facilitate success. We are at a great disadvantage unless we make a point of knowing and functioning according to those laws.

Often, the reason people fail is that they think that success stems from luck. Luck is unpredictable, but the laws of life make the outworking of life predictable. You are too valuable to live on chance. Your life is not a game. Wherever you are in life right now is a result of laws that you have implemented—or have *not* implemented, either because you don't know them or you aren't applying them. It's time to learn or relearn those laws and live according to them!

Thought: Everything in this world, including you, is designed to succeed.

Reading: Proverbs 16:3

—Day 9—

KEY PRINCIPLES OF SUCCESS, PART 2

"Do not overwork to be rich; because of your own understanding, cease! Will you set your eyes on that which is not? For riches certainly make themselves wings; they fly away like an eagle toward heaven." —Proverbs 23:4–5 (NKJV)

As I wrote on day 7 of this devotional, success is predictable because it is related to life's laws. We may experience challenges and setbacks, but if we keep following the laws of life, we will overcome our difficulties and emerge successful.

A corollary principle is that ignoring or disobeying the laws of life is predictive of failure. For example, if I uprooted a sapling and left it lying on the ground, can I predict what will happen to that plant? Yes. I can predict its failure to function as it was meant to, and unless I do something to help it, it will shrivel up and die. But if I plant a sapling in the soil and give it water and nutrients, can I also predict what will happen to it? Yes. I can predict its success. Your life is as simple as a plant, but it's also as complicated as a plant. The laws are simple, but we need to faithfully put them into practice. Otherwise, we will struggle throughout life.

Once more, success and failure in life are not mysterious. They are both related to laws.

Another principle to keep in mind is that success is not a pursuit in and of itself. Most people who "try" to be successful do not end up being successful. Are you trying to be successful? Are you trying to be great? Are you trying to be prosperous? It won't happen. Prosperity will run from you, a reality that is captured by the opening Scripture for today.

It is vital to have dreams, but the more you run after success, the more it runs from you. That is predictable because success isn't found that way. A car doesn't "try" to function well. Just give it what it needs for its engine and its other parts to work—just follow the laws that make cars run—and it will function well. It is the same with our life. We need to provide it with what it needs to function well. So, don't make success your ultimate aim. Instead, make it your goal to follow your dream and exercise your gift as you obey the laws of success.

Thought: Success is not an aim in and of itself. Success results from following your dream and exercising your gift according to the laws of success.

Reading: Micah 6:8

—Day 10—

OBEYING LIFE'S LAWS

"If you fully obey the Lord *your God and carefully follow all his commands I give you today, the* Lord *your God will set you high above all the nations on earth. All these blessings will come on you and accompany you if you obey the* Lord *your God...."* —Deuteronomy 28:1–2

If success is not a pursuit, then what is it? It is a *result* or *byproduct* of living in obedience to certain laws. People who are truly successful are simply adhering to certain laws and reaping the results.

Because of some negative connotations of the word, some people might not like the term *obey* when it comes to following laws. However, it simply means "to follow the commands or guidance of" or "to conform to or comply with."[1] We obey many laws of life every day without even realizing it. For example, when you eat a meal, you are voluntarily obeying a natural law that says your body needs nourishment to maintain life. Most people don't ignore that law because they know that obeying it will keep them alive. If they refuse to eat, they jeopardize their health. Similarly, obeying the laws of success will sustain you and enable you to thrive.

The two most common reasons for failure in life are therefore ignorance of laws and disobedience to laws. We need to put in the effort to activate life's laws. Obedience to the inherent laws of life is always in our best interests.

In this sense, we become what we decide to be. What I am today, I actually *made a decision* to become. We must learn to stop blaming other people for our state. Others may be responsible for

1. Merriam-Webster.com Dictionary, s.v. "obey," https://www.merriam-webster.com/dictionary/obey.

hurting you, which is another topic, but they aren't responsible for who you are or what you become. The only way to correct failure is to start following—or return to following—life's laws.

People keep expecting to succeed when they disregard the laws of success. Again, generally speaking, whatever we are right now, we made a choice to be. That includes being unfulfilled and unprosperous. But if you're not where you want to be, you can begin today to turn things around.

Once we implement a law, we can trust that law to go to work for us. Returning to yesterday's analogy of a plant, once you provide the soil, water, and nutrients, you can't do anything to make that plant grow. Your job is to support the laws of nature, and then growth occurs in the plant by an internal working out of those laws. Is there something with your name on it that has been waiting for you to activate a law so it can come into fulfillment?

Thought: Obeying—or living in accordance with—life's laws of success brings fulfillment and prosperity.

Reading: Galatians 6:7

—Day 11—

DESIGNED AND TESTED

"I praise you because I am fearfully and wonderfully made; your works are wonderful, I know that full well."

—Psalm 139:14

The laws of life have a relational aspect to them, and we need to be aware of this context to fully understand and implement them. I will now share with you one of my favorite illustrations that has helped many people over the years to comprehend this aspect and apply it in a variety of arenas, from leadership to personal relationships. It's an example from the world of manufacturing.

A manufacturer puts their name and/or logo on every product they make. Your shoes have a brand name inside them, and the name may also be stitched on the outside. Your shirt has a label with the company's name on it, and the name might also be featured on the front. Your car has a brand name affixed to the back of it (and elsewhere on the exterior and interior of the vehicle). Your phone has a company name or logo on it.

The name or logo on a product reflects its *image*. Apple Inc. has an image. Microsoft Corporation has an image. Ford has an image. Mercedes-Benz has an image. What's most important for us to understand is that, in the manufacturing process, *the last thing a manufacturer puts on a product is its image*. They place the image on their product only when they consider it finished.

Let me define "finished" for you. I'm talking about products, but, ultimately, I'm talking about the way we are designed as human beings. A manufacturer finishes making their product before they sell it. However, the company does not allow a product to leave their manufacturing plant until it has been *tested*. They pay people to test the product to make sure everything about it is working. After this process is complete, the company's image is placed on the item, and then the product is prepared for shipping. In this sense, when you purchase a new product, it's not technically brand-new—it has already been used in order to be tested. But only then can it be said to be "finished."

When a manufacturer allows a product to leave the plant, they are so sure the product will work that they include an owner's manual with it that contains a lot of promises. If the product is a phone, the user manual might say, "This device can be used to make phone calls." How do they know that for sure? They have already tested it. "This phone can connect to the Internet." How can they make that claim? They've already tested it. "This phone can send text messages." How can they guarantee it? They've tested it. "This phone's battery will last eight hours." How can they be sure? They've tested the battery to confirm its longevity. So again, when the manufacturer puts their image on it, that's a sign that the product is not at the beginning of the manufacturing process but at the very end. The imprint of their image signifies completion, and we will soon discover the implications of this truth for your own journey to success.

Thought: "Products" that are sent out into the world have been designed, tested, and proven to be effective. The same can be said of your life.

Reading: Isaiah 6:8

—Day 12—

GUARANTEED BY GOD

"This is what the Lord says—your Redeemer, the Holy One of Israel: 'I am the Lord your God, who teaches you what is best for you, who directs you in the way you should go.'"

—Isaiah 48:17

Continuing with our analogy of a product, we know that the accompanying owner's manual is a collection of laws prescribed by the manufacturer that should be followed by the consumer in order to guarantee that the product will function correctly. These laws are clearly not given to harm the product but to protect it and ensure its longevity.

At the back of an owner's manual, there is usually a page entitled, "Warranty." A warranty explains that the company fully backs its product. It says that if anything goes wrong with the item within a certain amount of time—if any deficiency exists, if it doesn't work—then, if you ship it back to them, they will pay for the shipment and repair the item at their expense. They will replace any defective parts with new parts directly from their own inventory. They will either ship the repaired product back to you, or they will replace the item with a completely new one (also having been tested)—all at their expense.

The people who run that company don't know you personally, so why would they spend all the money involved in either repairing or replacing a defective product? Why are they so dedicated to doing this? They aren't doing it because they like you, so there must be some other motivation for why they're so committed to it. The reason has nothing to do with you. The company does all of that for their own sake—for their *name's sake*. They are protecting their reputation in the marketplace because their name is on their product.

The owner's manual even warns you not to attempt to fix the product yourself. In other words, no one should try to fix someone else's product. That's a deep statement. Why? Because the company wants its success to be tied to its name. They know that if anything fails in this product, their entire reputation, the public's perception of their character, may be in trouble.

That's also why a company will voluntarily recall certain products and repair them at its own expense. The success of their product protects their reputation because they have put their name on it, and they have guaranteed that it works.

How does all this apply to our success? We have established the law that everything in life was designed to succeed. The next concept I would like to share is an expansion of that law: our success was designed by the Creator of the universe.

This truth has several implications, which we will explore in tomorrow's devotion.

Thought: Your success was designed by the Creator of the universe.

Reading: Psalm 121:1–2

—Day 13—

GOD'S IMAGE AND LIKENESS

"Then God said, 'Let us make mankind in our image, in our likeness, so that they may rule....'" —Genesis 1:26

God, the Creator of the universe, made a "product" called human beings. It was He who gave us our inherent purpose and gifts as elements of the divine part of our human makeup.

The word "*image*" in today's verse refers to the characteristics that God endued us with when He put His stamp, or His image, on us so that we would have His very character. The word "*likeness*" indicates that we are to function like Him. And God never fails; thus, every human being was created to succeed. God has never created a failure. People may fail, but that's not God's purpose and will for them.

The Creator had His own "manufacturing plant" where He tested human beings before He put His image on them. This means that you did not begin your life when God created you. Rather, your life started long before you were even conceived in your mother's womb.

Therefore, you can say to others, "What I am going to be, I already am. You just haven't seen it yet." Your purpose is built in. You came to earth because you are finished. When God released you to live on the earth, you arrived with everything you need to fulfill your purpose in life and to succeed.

Yesterday, we talked about owner's manuals. When you purchase a new appliance, do you read every page of the manual that comes with it? Probably not! That may be the reason you can't figure out why the product does certain things. The item may have twenty-five functions, but you know only four. You are not operating it according to all twenty-five facets of its potential. You are living below the product's ability to assist you.

Some of us do the same thing with our own potential for success. We know only four things: Get up and go to work, come home, eat dinner, and go to bed—day in and day out. We've gotten stuck because we have never heard of or closely followed the laws of creation that will make all the difference for us. Yet the Creator's Manual, the Bible, gives us specific laws to help us to better understand His nature and align with His purposes, to guide our relationship with Him and other people, and to enable us to be successful in fulfilling our inherent purpose. Knowing and following these laws enables us to be strong and bold, with no fear about life. This is possible when we recognize that God created us, that He designed us to succeed, and that our success is in His best interests.

Thought: When God released you to live on the earth, you arrived with everything you would need to fulfill your purpose in life and to succeed.

Reading: Jeremiah 1:1–10

—Day 14—
THE END FROM THE BEGINNING

"I make known the end from the beginning, from ancient times, what is still to come. I say, 'My purpose will stand, and I will do all that I please.'" —Isaiah 46:10

You were not born to figure out your life's purpose. You were born *with* your purpose already in place. Again, the problem may be that you're afraid of yourself and your dreams because your family or culture or government has told you who you can and can't be. (Or maybe you have placed limits on yourself regarding who you can be.) Yet you can't measure your worth against other human "products," because no one knows a product like its manufacturer. Those other products need to mind their own business and keep their thoughts to themselves because they don't know who you are.

The Creator would not have allowed you to begin unless you were already finished. In today's opening Scripture, we see that the Creator makes known what is yet to come because what is yet to come already came! God put inside you who you really are. He says, "When I show you what's ahead of you, you can see it. I will not allow you to see what does not already exist."

What can we conclude from this? We don't have to try to win in life anymore. We have already won; we are already successful and just need to manifest that success.

King David wrote in one of his psalms, *"Take delight in the Lord, and he will give you the desires of your heart"* (Psalm 37:4). Our dreams originate with God, who has placed His desires for us within our heart. The heart, in this case, means the subconscious mind. God put His plans there because He wants to make sure we find them.

Let's go back to our opening verse, where God said, *"My purpose will stand, and I will do all that I please."* In other words, "This is My purpose for your life. It's already finished, and it will stand." The word *"stand"* there doesn't mean that it's standing up. It means it won't go away—it will frustrate you until you do something about it. It means you will never be happy doing anything else. We cannot change what we were born to do and to be, and still be fulfilled and successful. Again, that purpose will always frustrate us until we act on it.

What you are created to be can be ignored or smothered, but it can never be changed. I believe you are a great man or woman, but what have you settled for in life? Have you allowed yourself to be reduced to a number at your job? Perhaps that is how people perceive you. But that's not the way God sees you. He sees you as someone with divine purpose who is a success.

Thought: You are already successful and just need to manifest that success.

Reading: Isaiah 46:11

—Day 15—

THE UNIVERSALITY OF LAWS

"If the ax is dull and its edge unsharpened, more strength is needed, but skill will bring success." —Ecclesiastes 10:10

There are some people who seem to despise laws of any kind. That's because they don't really understand the purpose of laws (at least good, sound ones): to guarantee functionality and also to protect.

Here's the application of today's Scripture: If you don't know and understand the Creator's laws and principles of success, you'll keep working hard, just as you have to do with a dull ax, but you still won't cut the "tree" down. You won't accomplish what you were born to do. You can work diligently and still not be a success, thus failing to reflect the Manufacturer's reputation.

Life is not just about working hard. It's about working skillfully, working smartly. Does your ax need sharpening? Are you merely working hard, or are you working smartly by putting life's laws and principles to work?

For example, the fact that a car needs to run on fuel (or perhaps a combination of fuel and electricity) is a "law" that is built into the vehicle. So, if you want what the manufacturer promises, then you must follow their principles. First, you must *know* what the principle is—in this case, that the car runs on fuel; second, you must *accept* or *submit to* the need to put fuel in your car; and, third, you must actually *put* fuel into your gas tank. This process of knowing, accepting, and taking action applies to all laws and principles and in many contexts.

Laws define the way life works. Of course, you can work contrary to a principle. For example, you can put orange juice instead of gasoline in your car, but that would cancel the manufacturer's promise. The law says your car needs gasoline, and that means you have to go where you can obtain that fuel: a service station. If, one day, you decide that you're no longer going to put gas in the tank of your car, your car will stop working and will cease to fulfill its purpose. Thus, laws create relationships. You relate to service stations for as long as you desire your car to keep functioning properly.

When you know life's laws and principles and learn to relate to them consistently, you no longer need to experiment or guess about what you should do. The result is that you can live life with fewer mistakes and keep moving in the right direction. So, life's laws are not something to avoid or escape. On the contrary, when we act in accordance with them, we can predict our success and even reduce our workload on the way to fulfilling our purpose.

Thought: Life's laws are accessible and even beneficial when you understand and work according to them.

Reading: Psalm 1:1–3

—Day 16—

KEY TRUTHS ABOUT LAWS

"Your [infinite] knowledge is too wonderful for me; it is high above me, I cannot reach it." —Psalm 139:6 (AMPC)

The Creator of life's laws truly has knowledge that is beyond our comprehension. Yet we have the ability to at least recognize many of the laws He has put in place for our protection and benefit. Here are some key truths about laws that we can identify and see played out in the world around us:

- *Laws are permanent.* They are time-tested and do not change like styles or fads do.
- *Laws are universal.* They work anywhere, similar to the physical law of gravity, which is at work around the world, all the time. Accordingly, if you learn the keys of God's kingdom, which are universal and permanent, you can use them no matter where you live. This means that you don't necessarily need to change your geographical location to be successful, although there may be times when a change of environment or location will be beneficial. But success will come looking for you if you follow the laws.
- *Laws work regardless of circumstances.* This means that they work whether things are going well or poorly in your life, your community, or your nation.
- *Laws are not partial—they don't show favoritism.* Laws don't work only for people of a particular race, nationality, or social status. To return to the example of physical laws, gravity pulls equally on people of all races and nationalities. Similarly, the laws of life work for all people if the people work the laws.

- *Laws guarantee results and success.* This means that you can actually steer what happens in your life from now on. If you seem to be failing, try to study what laws you may be violating. If you are succeeding, study the laws you are following so you can better understand your success and build on it.
- *Laws and principles protect the product from abuse.* God's laws protect the "products" He created and the purposes for which He created them. Protection comes in obedience to those laws. For example, when you stop at a red light, you don't need to worry about getting a traffic ticket. The protection is in obeying the law. Guilt comes when you break a law, because you're no longer protected by that law. Obedience to the laws of creation leads to a successful life.
- *Laws serve the product.* If you want success, it is to your benefit to work with laws and principles because they will serve your purpose in life.
- *Laws simplify product operation.* Once more, laws help to eliminate the guesswork on how we are to proceed in life.

I cover a number of the Creator's laws of success in this book, but you can read many more in His Manual. When some people think of God's laws, they think only of the Ten Commandments. Believe me, there are many more laws than that. There's really no end to learning them—and there's no limit to their benefits.

Thought: You can simplify your life by working with the laws of God's kingdom rather than against them.

Reading: Isaiah 40:8

—Day 17—

LAWS GUARANTEE FUNCTIONALITY

"I will give you the keys of the kingdom of heaven."
—Matthew 16:19

As we have said, the laws of life are given to guarantee our functionality (success), and they also protect us. Obedience to the laws of our Creator always supports and protects our best interests.

On many occasions, Jesus of Nazareth talked about the essential nature of the Creator's laws. At one point, when He was talking about living in God's kingdom, He said, *"The knowledge of the secrets of the kingdom of heaven has been given to you"* (Matthew 13:11). Those *"secrets"* He also called "keys": *"I will give you the keys of the kingdom of heaven, and whatever you bind* [lock up] *on earth will be bound* [locked up] *in heaven, and whatever you loose* [unlock] *on earth will be loosed* [unlocked] *in heaven"* (Matthew 16:19). We may have a key to a safety deposit box with $2 million in it, but because we don't know it, we're living as if we were broke.

Jesus said He would give us laws by which we can cause heaven to act on earth on our behalf. You can make things begin to happen, or you can stop things from happening, according to these laws. When you use the keys according to their intended purpose, in whatever you allow, heaven will back you up; in whatever you stop, heaven will back you up.

There is not just one "key" to the kingdom; there are *keys*—many of them. Why is this so important? Because Jesus said these keys open up heaven or close heaven. They open up life or close life. In other words, these keys determine whether you live a locked-up life or an open life. Whether you fail or succeed. And it's the keys that you obey that will open the way for a successful life. Notice that, in this context, Jesus says heaven will do what you do, which, once more, means that He's telling us that success is not up to God—it's up to us.

You can't put the laws and principles of the kingdom into effect, with God's help, unless you know the keys behind them. That's because, as a God of laws, our Creator responds to laws. Again, it is just as with any manufacturer: if you obey the laws of the manufacturer, they guarantee that the product will operate because they support their product. If you have ignored or resisted the Creator's laws in the past, won't you adopt and follow them today? Your success depends on it.

Thought: The keys of the kingdom will enable you to open the way for a successful life.

Reading: Psalm 19:8–11

—Day 18—

YOUR SUCCESS FOR GOD'S SAKE

"We have sinned, even as our ancestors did.... Yet he saved them for his name's sake, to make his mighty power known."

—Psalm 106:6, 8

We know that everything God created, He built for success: air, water, sky; fish, birds, mammals; atoms, cells, organs; men, women, children. When a tree grows from a seed, it is really not for the sake of the plant; it's for the sake of the Creator. Therefore, the success of a product is not good for the product itself—it's good for the manufacturer.

You can say to yourself, "My success is good for God!"

When I discovered this truth, it changed my life. When, from reading the Bible, I came to understand the principle that my success is good for God, I began to "put pressure" on God to fulfill what He had promised. We talked a few days ago about how a product carries with it the entire credibility of the manufacturer and its name. The Hebrew word for "name" is *seth,* and this term is very significant: "In Hebrew thought a name is never a mere label. It embodies identity, character, authority, memory, reputation, and destiny."[2]

In other words, in Hebrew, the name of a thing *is* the thing. In ancient times, a name was not just a label; it was a representation of character. This is why, when the great leader Moses asked God to tell him His name, it was a problem for God to answer that question. He told Moses, "Well, '*I am who I am*' (Exodus 3:14). That's what I am." Translated into English, it doesn't make sense.

---

2. "8034. shem," Topical Lexicon, Bible Hub, https://biblehub.com/hebrew/8034.htm.

We ask, "God, what is Your name?" God replies, "It depends on what I am at the time. Call Me that." You fill in the blank depending on what God is for you at that moment.

For example, God doesn't heal people; He *is* Jehovah Rapha, the God who Heals. God doesn't bring peace; He *is* Jehovah Shalom, the God of Peace. God doesn't provide things for you; He *is* Jehovah Jireh, the God Who Provides. Some people talk about wanting to know all the names of God, but that's impossible if He becomes whatever you need Him to be at the time. If you are sick, you don't need money—you need Jehovah Rapha. The person right next to you may need money. God becomes Jehovah Jireh to that person. So, you have two manifestations of God's character in the same place.

This same God became flesh and dwelt among us in a person called Yeshua—a name translated as Joshua, or Jesus, that simply means "Savior," even though He used a host of other names to refer to Himself. These names were meant to show us all He could do and be for us, His children. And our success is an outworking of His various helps in our lives.

Thought: Jesus is whatever you need Him to be in the moment, and your success is good for Him.

Reading: Ephesians 1:3–10

—Day 19—

ACTIVATING THE LAWS OF SUCCESS

"Anyone who sets aside one of the least of these commands and teaches others accordingly will be called least in the kingdom of heaven, but whoever practices and teaches these commands will be called great in the kingdom of heaven."

—Matthew 5:19

When you follow your purpose and obey the related laws, you will attract good things, such as opportunities and other benefits—and people will come seeking you. For example, I received a phone call from someone on the board of the NFL who said, "Look, we are having some problems with NFL players. They're having difficulties." He talked about how their marriages were breaking up, and how they were having issues in other areas. Then he said, "You're the man that we want to come in and talk to the players."

"Me?" I asked.

"Yes," he replied. "We've read some of your material. We want to retain you as a consultant."

Being a consultant for the NFL was not something I pursued, and it would have been unlikely to predict, given that I live on an island that is only seven miles wide and had never moved to a major metropolitan area to try to get a better job or to advance my career. Success and influence came looking for me when I wasn't even looking for them. All I was doing was continuing to follow the Creator's laws and principles that I had learned.

In today's opening Scripture, Jesus indicated that when you learn how important laws are, and when you practice them and teach them to others, you will become great.

God told Moses's successor, Joshua, the same secret to success: *"Be careful to obey all the law my servant Moses gave you; do not turn from it to the right or to the left, that you may be successful wherever you go. Keep this Book of the Law always on your lips; meditate on it day and night, so that you may be careful to do everything written in it. Then you will be prosperous and successful"* (Joshua 1:7–8). Notice that God put the responsibility of success on Joshua, not on Himself. God was saying, "If you keep My laws and obey My commands, if you do not turn from them to the right or to the left, I guarantee that you will make your way prosperous, and you will be successful."

I have underscored that both success and failure are predictable. So, you can actually reverse this statement: "If you do *not* keep this Book of the Law, then you will be unprosperous and unsuccessful."

Suppose you put a wheat seed on a tile floor and left it there for twenty years. You might pray over that seed, asking God to make it grow, but your prayers would not bring a wheat plant from a seed for which the conditions for growth were not met. Laws cannot be substituted for by prayer. Likewise, prosperity doesn't come by prayer alone but by keeping laws.

God doesn't answer prayer because we pray loudly or even emotionally. We have to come to Him with His keys. God is compassionate and forgiving, yet we cannot ignore His laws even as we look for His help and guidance.

Thought: Jesus indicated that when you learn how important laws are, and when you practice them and teach them to others, you will become great.

Reading: Matthew 5:1–10

—Day 20—

SHORTCUTS DELAY SUCCESS

> *"Seek first his kingdom and his righteousness* [or righteous laws], *and all these things* [everything needed for everyday life] *will be given to you as well."* —Matthew 6:33

The way to a successful life is order, or alignment with what God has purposed and planned, and order comes from law. Jesus indicated the same thing in the above verse. By using the word *"first,"* Jesus was indicating priority. He valued the kingdom, the influence of heaven on earth, more than anything else.

Sometimes, people expect the kingdom of God to work like magic. These people look for miracles all the time. When certain religious leaders asked Jesus for a miraculous sign, He replied, *"A wicked and adulterous generation asks for a sign!"* (Matthew 12:39). In other words, they were looking for shortcuts.

To take a shortcut means to go against a law or laws. Believe me, the longest way to success is the shortcut. In the writings of the New Testament, there are several accounts describing Jesus being tempted by Satan, or the devil. One of the greatest temptations the devil levied on Jesus was this one: he took Him to the highest pinnacle of the temple and said, "If You really are who You say You are—jump! You won't hurt Yourself—God's Word says that He will protect You." (See Matthew 4:5–6; Luke 4:9–11.)

The devil was telling Jesus to take a shortcut. "Don't go through all the pain and suffering of the crucifixion. Just get it over with. If You jump now and live, they'll believe in You." But Jesus answered, *"It is also written: 'Do not put the Lord your God to the test'"* (Matthew 4:7).

If you cut across somebody's yard instead of going along the main road, you call it a shortcut, don't you? But what are you really doing? Trespassing.

Jesus taught His disciples to pray, *"Forgive us our debts"* (Matthew 6:12), which is often expressed as, "Forgive us our trespasses." In other words, "God, forgive us for trying to quicken things in life by avoiding the process of following Your laws." This is why people get into problems in business, attempting get-rich-quick schemes. This is also why gambling is destructive—it encourages shortcuts to amassing wealth. We can't go against laws and not experience the consequences.

Don't take shortcuts to find your own way of doing things. The Creator has established laws in life for everyone to follow for the most successful results. Everybody else may think you are successful, but you may actually be failing because you haven't been doing what God has planned for your life. God has a future, a mark, ahead of you that's supposed to be what you reach. If you don't make it to the future God intended, no matter how many people have celebrated you along the way, you aren't a success because you haven't fulfilled your purpose. Ask the Lord to keep you on the proper path and to help you bypass the shortcuts!

Thought: There are no shortcuts to true success.

Reading: Jeremiah 9:23–24

—Day 21—

GROWTH FROM FOLLOWING LAWS AND PRINCIPLES

"Although the Lord gives you the bread of adversity and the water of affliction, your teachers will be hidden no more; with your own eyes you will see them. Whether you turn to the right or to the left, your ears will hear a voice behind you, saying, 'This is the way; walk in it.'" —Isaiah 30:20–21

God has given us the keys, principles, systems, and concepts by which we can have success. My desire is to help you see your purpose and align your life with that purpose so that you can be successful. Today we will talk about some ways in which following laws and principles enable us to develop personally, building us up so we can achieve success.

First of all, knowing laws and principles gives us peace and confidence because we understand the way forward and trust in the process of success, and we aren't discouraged by naysayers. I teach the laws and principles of success with full confidence because I have learned them, I have tested them, and I have personally proved them. I can affirm that these laws work.

Next, laws and principles embolden us because they are the enemies of fear. When you know the laws of life, you don't have to be afraid of negative circumstances because you understand that you can respond to them with the appropriate principles. Fear is often evidence of ignorance.

Jesus Christ had confidence and boldness even when facing death. This wasn't simply because He was God. It was because He had knowledge. He said, "My Father told Me that if I lay My life down, I can take it up again." (See John 10:17–18.) It was information that gave Him confidence and boldness. Knowing laws reduces and cancels fear.

A knowledge of laws and principles is also the source of wisdom. In the book of Proverbs, Solomon wrote, "*The beginning of wisdom is this: Get wisdom. Though it cost all you have, get understanding*" (Proverbs 4:7). Solomon was talking about laws here. If you understand laws, you become wise. Wisdom is the application of time-tested laws and principles. Three words we want to keep in mind are *knowledge, understanding,* and *wisdom*. Knowledge is information, and understanding is comprehension, but wisdom is application. You may actually know laws but not apply them. If so, the result will be the same as if you didn't know the laws: you will flounder and fail.

Laws and principles are more important than power because employing them is what leads to power. Someone who knows laws will find that they have various types of power related to exercising their purpose and gifting, just as Joshua discovered as he followed God's command to be strong and courageous by keeping the law.

Thought: Knowing and keeping God's laws and principles is the way to peace and confidence; boldness; wisdom; and power.

Reading: Luke 11:28

—Day 22—

NATURAL LAWS AND SPIRITUAL LAWS

"Through Christ Jesus the law of the Spirit who gives life has set you free from the law of sin and death." —Romans 8:2

As we follow the laws of the Creator while serving our gift, it's important to recognize how natural laws and spiritual laws are both similar to and different from one another. This will keep us from mistaking one for the other and enable us to effectively apply them. Let's begin today by discussing the distinctions of natural laws.

1. *Natural laws were established by the Creator.* For instance, no human being created the laws of gravity, motion, or thermodynamics. God's wonderful design of the universe created these things.
2. *Natural laws establish natural order.* The word *natural* is derived from the word *nature*. Thus, whatever is built into nature is what we call "natural"—it is generally the way things work in the created world.
3. *Natural laws regulate natural relationships.* We talked on an earlier day about how a tree is connected to the soil in which it is planted. The tree and the soil have a relationship according to natural law. There are many such natural relationships on earth. For example, we human beings don't produce oxygen ourselves, but it's a physical law that we need to breathe oxygen to live. Plants and trees produce oxygen, so we have a relationship with them; we must protect and nurture trees for our own sake. That's a relationship based on a law.

4. *Natural laws cannot be changed.* They are inherent in the environment of the created world.
5. *Natural laws have built-in ramifications or consequences depending on how we respond to them.* I mentioned previously how, if a tree were to be uprooted from the soil in which it was planted, we wouldn't have to guess what would happen to it. The judgment from its disconnection to what sustains it is built into the natural law governing it. Similarly, a fish has a relationship with water; it needs to live in water to survive. If a fish were to jump out onto dry land, it would soon suffer the consequences of that disconnection.

Similarly, if a human being were to try to defy a natural law, such as gravity, by jumping from a great height, they would probably be killed or at least critically injured. Once more, what this tells us is that success—and failure—is predictable when we understand laws.

Thought: Natural laws govern our existence in much the same way that spiritual laws do.

Reading: Psalm 147:4, 8–9

—Day 23—

THE NATURE OF SPIRITUAL LAWS

"For the wages of sin is death, but the gift of God is eternal life in Christ Jesus our Lord." —Romans 6:23

Let's now look at the nature of spiritual laws and how they are similar to and different from natural laws.

1. *Spiritual laws were established by the Creator,* just as natural laws were.
2. *There are spiritual laws that are inherent in the human spirit.* All of us, whether or not we believe in a Creator, generally know when we're doing something we shouldn't do. This is because there is a spiritual law within our being called the *conscience.*
3. *Spiritual laws regulate supernatural relationships.* For you to relate to God, you have to obey some spiritual laws, the first of which is submission. God can't help you if you don't yield to Him. Second, you have to confess to Him that you don't know anything! That's a spiritual law. You can't go to God as if you have no need for Him.
4. *Spiritual laws are eternal.* They are not limited to the laws of the finite world; they transcend nature.
5. *Spiritual laws have built-in ramifications or consequences.* Like natural laws, spiritual laws have their own inherent results. If we obey these laws, we reap positive consequences. If we disobey them, we reap negative consequences. When our forefather, Adam, decided to defy the Creator's law, the Creator didn't punish him with death—death was built into the law he had violated. (See Genesis

2:16–17.) So, just like a tree being uprooted from the soil where it is planted, or a fish leaping into an environment without water, when people decided to leave God, they spiritually died and, eventually, physically died. The relationship was determined by the laws that were set in place at the beginning of creation. That's why God sent Jesus to earth to restore the connection between human beings and Himself—so we could be given new life and be able to follow His laws of life once more.

6. *Spiritual laws can overrule natural ones.* There are times when the Creator will act in a way that is contrary to natural laws in order to carry out His purposes on earth. Physical laws have been established for the normal course of life on earth, and they hold true in that context. However, when spiritual laws enter the picture, natural laws are not necessarily invariable. For example, to allow the Israelites to escape from the pursuing Egyptians, God parted the Red Sea (see Exodus 14:21–22); when this occurred, the waters seemed to function against the law of gravity. In another example, Jesus walked on water (see Matthew 14:22–23), which, for a human being, isn't physically possible from a natural law standpoint. This is where God's supernatural laws override natural laws.

Thought: For you to relate to God, you have to obey some spiritual laws, the first of which is submission.

Reading: Isaiah 40:13–14

—Day 24—

MAXIMUM FULFILLMENT OF PURPOSE AND POTENTIAL

"For in [God] *we live and move and have our being."*
—Acts 17:28

The laws of the Creator are both natural and supernatural, both physical and spiritual, to guarantee the maximum fulfillment of our purpose and potential. In other words, God created all the laws to work in our favor. Once more, the problem many people have in life is simple: they don't know the laws. So, they approach life experimentally, hoping things will work out for them.

My purpose and work are to teach, consult, and advise people, and I consider my role to be clear and straightforward: I help people understand laws. It isn't anything mysterious or complex. Laws don't take into account personal opinion. Whenever I give people advice, I focus on laws rather than my opinion. God's laws are not suggestions. They are instructions, and we want to receive His instructions.

The concept of need is related to laws. We don't "want" God—we *need* God. That's the reason many people come back to the Creator and His purposes. When we find out who He is, then we want Him because we learn what He is truly like. People think that coming to God is a religious experience. But it's actually about coming to our senses. Plants need soil. Fish need water. People need the Creator.

Jesus taught that, without God, we can do nothing. (See John 15:5.) Without soil, plants can do nothing. Without water, fish can do nothing. Without God, we can do nothing. This is not a matter of choice; it's a matter of order that is built into the laws of life and creation.

Humans are the only created beings who willfully and intentionally question, challenge, walk away from, and go against spiritual and natural laws. Fish never willingly leave water. Plants never willingly leave the soil. They don't challenge the law. Challenging these laws puts us in a predicament. That's why we are seeing forms of failure all over the world—people by the billions failing because they either don't know natural and spiritual laws or they intentionally act in a way that is contrary to them.

Remember that God told Moses's successor, Joshua, "If you obey My laws, you will be successful and prosperous." (See Joshua 1:7–8.) One Bible version translates the ending phrase as "*you will have good success*" (Joshua 1:8 NKJV). That expression "*good success*" reminds us that we can have bad success. A drug dealer may have a lot of money, but he probably can't sleep at night. Why? There may be people who are out to kill him, so he has to stay up all night guarding his money. That is not prosperity. That is torment.

Thought: Good success results from your obedience to the natural and spiritual laws that the Creator has established.

Reading: Psalm 62:5–8

—Day 25—

LAWS IMPART CONTROL

"A man reaps what he sows. Whoever sows to please their flesh, from the flesh will reap destruction; whoever sows to please the Spirit, from the Spirit will reap eternal life."

—Galatians 6:7–8

Jesus made a simple comment in a parable that is well-known but not fully understood by many people: "*A man scatters seed on the ground. Night and day, whether he sleeps or gets up, the seed sprouts and grows, though he does not know how. All by itself the soil produces grain—first the stalk, then the head, then the full kernel in the head*" (Mark 4:26–28). Jesus didn't say, "A man scatters seed on the ground, then goes to bed, worrying and praying about that seed; he gets up and strives to make that seed grow, saying, 'Seed, germinate!'" No, He indicated that the man plants the seed, then goes about his days; meanwhile, the seed grows and develops on its own. In other words, after sowing the seed, the man doesn't think about it anymore; he reasons, "I've done what I'm supposed to do. I've obeyed the laws. I can go to sleep at night without worrying about it." He knows the harvest is coming. This is what I mean when I say that laws give us peace and confidence.

This is difficult for many people because they want to "help" the Creator. They feel like if they aren't doing something, then they aren't doing anything. Yet Jesus says, "No, once you plant, you go to sleep." Why? Because, as I mentioned previously, the laws work automatically once you engage them. Once you obey them, they have their own internal productivity. They begin to produce.

To use another illustration from the automotive world, if you go to the service station and fill your car's fuel tank with gasoline, do you then pray for the car to have fuel so it can run? No. You have obeyed the law that your car functions on gasoline, so now you just start the engine, press the gas pedal, and go along your way.

Thus, when you know and obey the laws of life, you control the outcome. I'm not implying that we shouldn't submit our plans to the Creator and talk with Him about our concerns and decisions. But I am saying that we shouldn't just hope something works out rather than putting God's laws into practice—laws that He has already established for us to employ for our success.

The Creator has given us an Owner's Manual—the Bible—filled with the laws of life and creation. He gave us these laws so we would know what it means to live according to His nature and ways. Yet God's desire was not to have His laws recorded merely on stone or even paper. God revealed His ultimate plan with these words to the prophet Jeremiah: *"I will put my law in their minds and write it on their hearts"* (Jeremiah 31:33).

Thought: If we put God's laws into practice, we can have peace and confidence, expecting a good, godly outcome from our plans and pursuits.

Reading: Job 5:8

—Day 26—
LAWS VERSUS RULES

> *"Woe to you, teachers of the law and Pharisees, you hypocrites! You are like whitewashed tombs, which look beautiful on the outside but on the inside are full of the bones of the dead and everything unclean. In the same way, on the outside you appear to people as righteous but on the inside you are full of hypocrisy and wickedness."* —Matthew 23:27–28

Once we understand the foundations of the Creator's laws and their relationship to success, it's essential to make a distinction between a law and a "rule." We can't afford to confuse one with the other. Knowing the distinction eliminates frustration and confusion. Following the laws of life is the bedrock of success, but following "rules" can actually prevent you from being successful. A lack of success is, in many cases, due to the fact that someone has been obeying the rules. Anyone who wants to be successful must break some rules!

To contrast the two concepts, in today's devotion, we will briefly review the nature of the laws of life, and tomorrow we will look at the nature of rules.

One of the reasons I talked about the qualities of natural laws and spiritual laws, as I did on day 22, is that it helps us to see the differences between laws and rules. We know that laws are the inherent or built-in principles that regulate life and relationships within creation. This means:

- *True laws and principles can never be broken.* We don't "break" laws, even though we often use that terminology to describe acting against a law. In other words, when we disobey a law, it doesn't have an effect on the law—the law remains intact. Instead, it has an effect on us and our life.

- *True laws and principles break those who go against them.* Again, if you were to jump from the top of a ten-story building, you wouldn't violate gravity—gravity would violate you. You wouldn't push yourself down; gravity would pull you down.
- *The Creator does not have to impose judgment when we go against His laws and principles.* Once more, we make this conclusion based on the first two points. It is what I mean by laws having inherent judgment built into them.
- *True laws and principles attract and activate their own rewards when they are put into practice.* This is why I have said that failure or success is not up to God. God has finished establishing natural and spiritual laws. He created everything and put the laws in motion. It is up to us to follow them to be successful.

Thought: Anyone who wants to be successful must break certain rules.

Reading: Matthew 23:23–26

—Day 27—

THE NATURE OF RULES

"'I have the right to do anything,' you say—but not everything is beneficial. 'I have the right to do anything'—but I will not be mastered by anything. You say, 'Food for the stomach and the stomach for food, and God will destroy them both.' The body, however, is…for the Lord, and the Lord for the body."

—1 Corinthians 6:12–13

Now consider the points we covered yesterday in contrast to rules, which we could also refer to as traditions. People sometimes think of laws and rules as being the same thing, yet success requires keeping the law even while violating certain traditions.

When Jesus talked about our becoming great by practicing and teaching the commands of the law, He also said, *"For I tell you that unless your righteousness surpasses that of the Pharisees and the teachers of the law, you will certainly not enter the kingdom of heaven"* (Matthew 5:20). What does it mean to have "righteousness"? It simply means to be aligned with God's laws. Jesus is talking here about the difference between following tradition and obeying laws. He addressed this issue many times in His ministry.

Later on, some religious leaders asked Jesus, *"Why do your disciples break the tradition of the elders?"* (Matthew 15:2). Whose tradition were they speaking about? They were referring to the tradition of the elders, not of God. Thus, you must separate what human beings have established from what God has established. Not everything that humans have established is wrong. Some of it has been built upon the laws and principles of success that the Creator has put into place. But I guarantee you with all my strength that following man-made traditions and rules as your ultimate guide will undermine your purpose and lead to failure.

Jesus responded to the religious leaders in this way: "*Why do you break the command of God for the sake of your tradition?*" (verse 3). In other words, "Why do you break the laws of God in order to follow your rules?" This difference between laws and rules is vital for us to remember throughout life in order to keep fulfilling our purpose and attain success.

Thought: Obeying the law as a means to success is not necessarily the same as following tradition.

Reading: Isaiah 56:10–11

—Day 28—

POTENTIAL DANGERS OF RULES

"And why do you break the command of God for the sake of your tradition? For God said, 'Honor your father and mother' and 'Anyone who curses their father or mother is to be put to death.' But you say that if anyone declares that what might have been used to help their father or mother is 'devoted to God,' they are not to 'honor their father or mother' with it. Thus you nullify the word of God for the sake of your tradition." —Matthew 15:3–6

Several dictionary definitions of *law*[3] give us insights into the difference between laws and rules. Let's take a look at them:

1. "The revelation of the will of God set forth in the Old Testament"; "the first part of the Jewish scriptures: pentateuch, torah." The Pentateuch is the first five books in the Bible: Genesis, Exodus, Leviticus, Numbers, and Deuteronomy. These definitions of *law* would include many of the laws of God. The rules of men that are contrary to the Creator's laws will inevitably make people fail, keeping them from true prosperity and success.
2. "A binding custom or practice of a community: a rule of conduct or action prescribed or formally recognized as binding or enforced by a controlling authority." People call this "law," but it's actually a rule if it is based only on people's custom or practice rather than on the laws of creation.

3. Merriam-Webster.com Dictionary, s.v. "law," https://www.merriam-webster.com/dictionary/law.

This kind of "law" can be dangerous, such as the rules that governed the sale of human beings as slaves in America until the mid-1800s. The whole concept was supported by a rule created by the community, and it was binding and enforceable by a controlling authority. Some human rules are designed to restrict and control other human beings. They are imposed on people to retard their power.

What happened to abolish slavery in America? There were people who rose up and said, "We are against that rule because there's a higher law. There's a divine law that says that all humans are created equal, and that they are all made in God's image." Where did they get that law? From the book of Genesis and other parts of the Bible. The law became more important than the rule, and slavery was eventually abolished. You can see why man-made rules are not to be trusted implicitly.

3. "A command or provision enacted by a legislature." This may be the definition with the most frightening ramifications. People are enacting all kinds of laws today that I call rules because they are based on mere man-made ideas and are contrary to the laws of God.

How might you be mistaking a rule for a law in your own life?

Thought: We must weigh man-made rules against the universal laws of the Creator.

Reading: Colossians 2:20–23

—Day 29—

DIFFERENCES BETWEEN LAWS AND RULES, PART 1

"But now we are released from the law, having died to that which held us captive, so that we serve in the new way of the Spirit and not in the old way of the written code."

—Romans 7:6 (ESV)

In light of the definitions and the properties of the Creator's laws that we covered in yesterday's devotion, we can come to certain conclusions:

Laws are more important than rules. They were established in creation and are unchanging. They supersede rules.

Laws are different from rules. Laws are permanent, while rules are temporary and formulated on the consensus of members of a community, legislature, or other ruling authority.

Rules are man-made customs and boundaries. Human beings were designed by God to live according to, and to protect, natural law and divine law. What humanity has essentially attempted to do is to create a third set of laws, one of its own. Many times, these laws go against (or attempt to go against) the first two sets of laws. When people institute such rules, they create limitations for other people.

Laws should never be subject to rules. Martin Luther King Jr. said these words when he was fighting against the oppression of white domination in America: "There are two types of laws: There are just laws and there are unjust laws. I would be the first to advocate obeying just laws. One has not only a legal but a moral responsibility to obey just laws. Conversely, one has a moral responsibility to disobey unjust laws."[4]

Where there is conflict between a law and a rule, obey the law. There comes a point when we cannot allow laws to be subject to rules if we are going to fulfill our purpose and be successful. That might even mean going to jail. Martin Luther King Jr. went to prison because he broke the rule that says people are unequal. He acted in accordance with a higher law that says all people are equal. Obeying the law and breaking the rule came with a price that he was willing to pay.

Thought: God's laws supersede man-made rules. When there is a conflict between the two, we must be willing to break the rule in order to keep the law.

Reading: Acts 5:27–29

---

4. Martin Luther King Jr., "Martin Luther King Jr. on Just and Unjust Laws," John F. Kennedy Presidential Library and Museum, https://www.jfklibrary.org/sites/default/files/2020-04/Birmingham%20Letter%20Excerpts%20for%20Activity.pdf.

—Day 30—

DIFFERENCES BETWEEN LAWS AND RULES, PART 2

"God…has made us sufficient to be ministers of a new covenant, not of the letter but of the Spirit. For the letter kills, but the Spirit gives life." —2 Corinthians 3:5–6 (ESV)

I would like to make two further observations on the differences between laws and rules. First, *successful people always break rules for the sake of laws.* I remember when it was said that no man could break the four-minute mile. It was an unwritten rule, not a natural law, that a human being couldn't run a mile in a faster time than four minutes. Then, one man named Roger Bannister decided, "I'm going to break that rule." Once he broke it, many others broke it as well. Leaders are always rule-breakers. That's why they're leaders. You can't lead by keeping rules. You lead by keeping laws.

People create various types of rules all the time. Many people once believed that a computer had to be as big as a room because that's what computers were originally like. Then came such innovations as the desktop computer, the handheld computer, the wrist computer, and the eyeglasses computer. People keep breaking the rules made by men. If you want to be successful, find a rule to break. Some of these rules are technological and some are social and cultural. For example, some people believe that a person of a particular background, education, or culture can't do or achieve certain things. They have established certain rules for who is able (or allowed) to be successful in various aspects of life. Somebody is going to come along and break those rules because they are man-made.

It is important for you to *never be afraid to break the rules for the sake of the law of God in creation.* I believe rules by men were made to be broken. Only those who break them make history.

Suppose you have a *job* in a hotel, but the God-given dream within you is to *own* a hotel. You may think, or you may hear someone say, "You could never own a hotel; you come from a poor family." Who is telling you that you can't do it? Whoever it is, they are making the rules of men more important than the laws of God, just like the religious leaders in Jesus's day. You have to settle the issue of which you are going to follow: rules or laws. Sometimes we make up rules for ourselves that have no basis in the laws of life. Remember, exercising laws leads to confidence and boldness, not fear.

Thought: We should never be afraid to break the rules for the sake of the law of God in creation.

Reading: Daniel 3:13–18

—Day 31—

LAWS AND RULES ACCORDING TO JESUS

"[Jesus said to the Pharisees,] '*So for the sake of your tradition you have made void the word of God. You hypocrites! Well did Isaiah prophesy of you, when he said: "This people honors me with their lips, but their heart is far from me; in vain do they worship me, teaching as doctrines the commandments of men."*'" —Matthew 15:6–9 (ESV)

The following are several statements by Jesus of Nazareth that we can apply to obeying laws and breaking rules:

"*Everything is possible for one who believes*" (Mark 9:23). To do the "impossible," we must believe in God's laws over man's rules. Success begins by ignoring and violating human rules and limitations.

Jesus also said, "*Therefore I tell you, whatever you ask for in prayer, believe that you have received it, and it will be yours. And when you stand praying, if you hold anything against anyone, forgive them, so that your Father in heaven may forgive you your sins*" (Mark 11:24–25). When we are following the Creator's laws that govern life and relationships, we can be assured that He will support us in exercising the gift He has placed within us.

"*The knowledge of the secrets of the kingdom of heaven has been given to you, but not to them*" (Matthew 13:11). Others have their rules, but you have the laws of the kingdom. Remember that Jesus also said, "*I will give you the keys of the kingdom of heaven, and whatever you bind* [lock up] *on earth will be bound* [locked up] *in heaven, and whatever you loose* [unlock] *on earth will be loosed* [unlocked] *in heaven*" (Matthew 16:19). Every time you come across a man-made lock, know that you have the keys to unlock it.

Successful people know the laws that unlock the locks of men. People will try to lock you up and lock you down. They will tell you that you can't do what you're meant to do. They might say, "You could never be a clothes designer. There's too much competition in the fashion industry." God says, "No, I have given you the vision and the gifts to be a clothes designer, and I will show you how to make it happen."

I was never supposed to be able to do what I'm doing. What I have accomplished, I had to do by violating man-made rules. So, I want to encourage you: break some rules!

Thought: God has given us the keys we need to unlock man-made barriers standing in our way to success.

Reading: Revelation 1:17–18

—Day 32—

PRINCIPLES OF PURPOSE

"Many are the plans in a person's heart, but it is the Lord's purpose that prevails." —Proverbs 19:21

The *New King James Version* of the Bible translates the latter part today's verse like this: *"the Lord's counsel—that will stand."* You may have all sorts of plans for your life—what you want to do, where you want to go, what you want to build, and so forth. But God says, "Look, I have a purpose for your life that will make you the most fulfilled and successful." We can learn three things from Proverbs 19:21:

1. *Purpose precedes plans.* Before you were even alive to start making plans, God had a purpose in mind for your life.
2. *Purpose is more important than plans.* Some of your current plans might already align with God's purpose, but you must make a point of evaluating them in light of the purpose and gifting He has given you, and you should be open to altering them if needed.
3. *Purpose is more powerful than plans.* Why is this the case? God says, "My purpose will prevail over your plans."

We established earlier that God doesn't start anything until He's "finished" it, so you're already finished. You have big dreams within you because you're seeing your end. The Scriptures say that Jesus endured the cross—with its accompanying criticism, maligning, and shame—and fulfilled His purpose because He saw His end, or *"the joy that was set before Him"* (Hebrews 12:2 NKJV). He saw Himself sitting on the throne, reigning. I wonder what you see. Stop being afraid of what you dream of accomplishing.

When I was forty years old, I told my father, "I want to travel around the world, and I want to advise governments." My father asked, "Do you believe this is possible, son?" I said, "Yes." He replied, "Then I don't know how, but you must believe it." My father shared the perspective of Jacob, the father of Joseph, whose story is found in the Bible.

As a seventeen-year-old, Joseph had two dreams in which he saw his family members—including his father, mother, and eleven brothers—bowing down to him. At that time, Joseph was just a shepherd boy tending his family's sheep. But his dreams gave him a vision of his God-given purpose, or "end." He didn't know any of the details of that purpose, and when he described the dreams to his family, his brothers were jealous, while his father rebuked him for his apparent sense of self-importance. However, the record also says that *"his father kept the matter in mind"* (Genesis 37:11). Jacob didn't dismiss the matter because he had personal experience with dreams related to the purposes of God. Good parents don't kill their children's dreams—they feed those dreams, recognizing them as potential markers of purpose.

Thought: God has a purpose for your life, one for which He started making plans long before you were born.

Reading: Psalm 71:6

—Day 33—

SEEING PAST CURRENT CIRCUMSTANCES

> *"The Lord does not look at the things people look at. People look at the outward appearance, but the Lord looks at the heart."*
> —1 Samuel 16:7

Let me ask you again to take an honest look at where you are at this stage in your life. Perhaps your dream is not what you are doing right now. Your current job may not be what you feel called to do. If where you are now is not where you know God is drawing you, just remember that your current role is only temporary. In this section of the devotional, we will cover a number of principles of success for work and jobs.

Even if you feel that you are doing well financially or professionally, do you sense that there is still something missing or that what you are doing is incomplete? Don't stay parked where you are. Get back to your dreams. God is telling you that you can start again—right now. Maybe you dreamed of traveling the world or of running a business that helps other people in some way. Note that God is only obligated to finance His own programs. If you pursue your God-given dream, the rest—including the finances—will follow.

Think about how humbly King David got his start. God told the prophet Samuel to go to the home of Jesse in Bethlehem because a king lived there. Samuel was instructed to anoint this individual. So Samuel went to Jesse and said, "The Lord says there's a king in this house—the next king of Israel." Jesse told Samuel, "I have twelve sons." So Samuel said, "Bring them all out." Let's imagine the scene. The first one who comes out is a tall, commanding-looking young man. But Samuel says, "No, that's not him." The second son is strikingly handsome, but Samuel says, "No, that's not the one." The third is well-educated. No. The fourth is muscular. No. Everybody comes out looking good, but being the king wasn't their purpose. After Jesse presents son number eleven, he says, "Well, that's it. Everybody's accounted for." The prophet says, "None of them is the king, but the Lord says there is a king in this house somewhere."

Jesse replies, "I don't have any more sons." Then he suddenly says, "Well, there's still my youngest son, but he's the dirtiest and the smelliest, out tending the sheep." The prophet had him sent for, and as soon as he saw him, the Lord said, *"Rise and anoint him; this is the one"* (1 Samuel 16:12).

Yes, the future king of Israel was trapped inside a shepherd boy. Are you the forgotten one in your family? No one knows your greatness. You may be trapped in the wilderness with the sheep, but I have come to pour oil on your head and tell people that they don't know who you really are. They thought you were the least in your family and would never amount to anything, that you'd get a job and die paying a mortgage. God says nothing like it. You're a business owner, a writer, an artist, a governmental official, a scientist, a teacher, the leader of a nonprofit organization. There's a king or queen sitting in your chair!

Thought: Even if your dreams seem out of reach, God has a purpose for you that's bigger than your current situation.

Reading: 1 Corinthians 1:26–29

—Day 34—

YOUR JOB VERSUS YOUR WORK

"Whatever you do, do your work heartily, as for the Lord and not for people." —Colossians 3:23 (NASB)

To pursue your purpose and be successful, you must understand that there's a big difference between your job and your work. Never mistake one for the other.

- Your job is your skill. Your work is your gift.
- Your job is what people pay you to do. Your work is what you were born to do.
- Your job is your career. Your work is your life assignment.
- Your job gives you benefits. Your work gives you fulfillment.
- Your job gives you a salary. Your work gives you prosperity.

For many people, especially when there is an economic downturn, a fear of losing their job is one of their greatest concerns. I want to address this fear because I believe that our concept of a job is where the problem lies. Suppose you were laid off from your job or were given fewer work hours. If you have placed your hope in your job, then you will probably feel like your future is in jeopardy because your means of living is being threatened. *But no job, in itself, has a future in it. Instead, the future is in the one who holds the job.*

Our culture has not trained us to find our gift—it has trained us to find a job. It's as if we believe we were born to be employed. Our economic psychology has made us dependent on the idea of having a job. But a job is really an opportunity someone else offers you. And if somebody offers you an opportunity, they can always take it back. If you build your life on someone else's offer, you are as safe as how they feel at the time, and they can change the way they feel at any point and withdraw that offer.

Don't ever allow an organization or a job to be your hope. For example, we are told, "Go learn a skill and apply for a position." The issue is, a skill is dispensable. That skill might become obsolete, or someone else who has the same skill might be hired for the position instead of you. No matter how much your company may praise and love you, you still need to think beyond your position because, if money becomes tight for that business or you get to a certain age, they may tell you goodbye.

This is why it is essential to ask, "What is my gift?" and really study that question. Because, when you discover your true work, you're not afraid to lose your job—you know there's life after it. You may be laid off or fired from a job, but you can never be laid off or fired from your work. Your job might be taken away from you, but no one can ever take your work away from you. You company can take away your ability to perform a certain skill, but they can't take away your gift. They can take away your activity, but they can't take away your ability.

Thought: No job, in itself, has a future in it. Instead, the future is in the one who holds the job.

Reading: Proverbs 18:16

—DAY 35—

ARE YOU EMPLOYED OR DEPLOYED?

"And whatever you do, whether in word or deed, do it all in the name of the Lord Jesus, giving thanks to God the Father through him." —Colossians 3:17

In yesterday's devotion, we talked about the difference between our job and our work. We saw that someone might take our job away from us, but they can never take our gift or our work away from us. If you took a fish out of a stream and put it in a pond, have you taken away its ability to swim? No, the gift went with the fish, even though you "fired" it from the stream. Remember, when you leave a job, your gift goes with you! While your skills may be dispensable, your gift is permanent. So, if you are ever laid off or fired, remember that you carry your gift with you, and, wherever you land, keep on swimming. Your employer didn't take your gift away from you—just the location in which you were using that gift.

This is why we need to change our thinking about our goal in life: we must think beyond a job. We must change our perspective about it and not let fear control us—we need to become free from the "spirit of jobs" so we can ignite the "spirit of work." And we start this process by understanding an important distinction between employment and deployment:

Employment means somebody else controls your life.

Deployment means you release what's inside you.

Deployment activates your gift and energizes your life. Always keep in mind that prosperity is not in your job; it is in your work—your gift, your assignment, what you were born to do. This is how you should think: "I was not born to be *employed*—I was born to be *deployed*."

Employment is the opportunity to serve your gift corporately, or in the context of a group, within a certain structure and oversight. But *deployment*—actively living out your purpose—is discovering your gift and serving that gift to the world and to your generation. Serving your gift to the world is also ultimately accomplished in conjunction with other people. Yet when you deploy yourself, it is because you have found something that is so sweet to do that you initiate your own activity, and others are drawn to it.

For those who are employed, their value is determined by the one who employs them. But those who deploy themselves determine their own value. In this context, by "value," I don't mean their intrinsic value, which they always have as human beings made in the Creator's image and likeness. Instead, I mean the way in which they are viewed and compensated. A salary is really someone else's opinion of how much you are worth. When you deploy yourself, you can establish your own worth. And those who deploy themselves often employ other people. They always benefit others in some way. If you're tired of being merely employed, focus on being deployed!

Thought: Deployment activates your gifts. It's the juice that makes you get up in the morning. It energizes your life.

Reading: 1 Peter 4:10–11

—Day 36—

WHEN YOUR JOB AND YOUR WORK DON'T MATCH

"The joy of the Lord *is your strength."* —Nehemiah 8:10

When people's jobs don't match their true work, and when they don't understand their purpose in life, it causes them all kinds of problems, including unhappiness, dissatisfaction, boredom, and bitterness.

Somebody who is in a place where they're not supposed to be is never comfortable. They can even feel tormented there because they're not built for it. Such a person's job is essentially suffocating their real gift. They are restricted by what the job tells them they can and can't do. They're always looking for the workday to end because they feel like a bird trapped in a cage for eight hours (or more).

You, too, may be going to a place or working a job from home every day that doesn't allow you to become who you are. The "cage" you are in confines you. A cage allows a bird to fly only within certain limitations. You're still a bird, and you still have the ability to fly high in the sky for miles on end, but you're in a cage. Your ability hasn't left. It's the restrictions that are holding you back. You are told, "This is as far as you can go." You could be trapped in this way for years. If this is your situation, you might always feel irritated or discouraged because you are continually in a place you don't want to be.

Many people who are unhappy at work spend years being merely employed while disturbing everybody else around them with their complaints, saying things like the following: "I don't know why I come here; this is a lousy job." "Management doesn't know what I'm worth." "They don't understand me." "I hate this place." "I'm supposed to get a promotion and a raise. Why is that not happening?" "I'm tired of being here; I want to go home." For ten years, they've been complaining about their job, but still they won't leave.

People's complaints may come from the fact that, because their gift is not being activated, there's no excitement or energy in their lives, and they feel frustrated and angry. In contrast, it's a pleasure to be around someone who is meant to be sitting next to you in your workplace. They are happy and excited to be there, and they help to create a positive environment.

When your job is in a place where you feel your creative and/or analytical juices flowing, and where you can release all the desires and gifts within you so that you are deploying your gift, then you can't wait to get there. As a matter of fact, it can be depressing when you reach the end of the day because you don't want to leave! A person who is functioning in their gift wants the days to be longer because they desire to keep doing what they're doing.

Thought: Your true work will make you feel your creative and/or analytical juices flowing and will enable you to release the desires and gifts within you.

Reading: 1 Thessalonians 1:3

—Day 37—

WORK IS NOT A CURSE

"The Lord God took the man and put him in the Garden of Eden to work it and take care of it." —Genesis 2:15

If your job is wearing you out, if it isn't the work that you envisioned, and if you keep watching the clock, waiting for the day to be over, then these are strong signs that you are not yet in your true work. The same may be true if you have experienced a certain degree of success in your place of employment, and you enjoy your job for the most part, but you feel you have reached a plateau, finding yourself restless or bored at times, sensing that there is more within you that is untapped.

I challenge you once more to think about where you are in your life, and at your present age—whether you are young, middle-aged, or older. Consider your current situation in relation to what you are discovering in this devotional. Ask yourself, "What's happening to my life? How many more years might I have left to fulfill my purpose?"

You have to activate your gift. Therefore, tap into your hidden seed, your treasure. When you're deployed, you serve your natural gift to the world, and the world pays you for being yourself. Can you imagine being paid for something you like to do?

Many people have difficulty understanding their purpose because they consider work itself to be a burden or a curse. This perspective can come from a misunderstanding of the biblical record. When human beings decided to act in a way that was contrary to the Creator's law, they had to leave the garden of Eden, and work became more difficult for them. (See Genesis 3:17–19.) But work itself is not a punishment from God. Work was established at the *beginning* of creation, before human beings went against God's law. The first book of Moses tells us that, after God created Adam, the first thing He instructed him to do was to work: *"The LORD God took the man and put him in the Garden of Eden to work it and take care of it"* (Genesis 2:15). The Hebrew word for *"work"* here is *ergon,* which can mean "to cause to exist, produce."[5] Some Bible versions translate *ergon* as *"cultivate"* and *"tend."* God instructed us to work because we were created to produce. That has not changed.

So, work is an established law in creation—the law of work. Whatever stops you from working is violating this law. If you want to get something for free or without making an effort, you're violating this law. Jesus of Nazareth said, *"My food...is to do the will of him who sent me and to finish his work"* (John 4:34). His *"food"*—the sustenance of His being—was to do the will of His Father. That's a vital statement. His work was to do what? The will. What does *"the will"* refer to? The intent of the Manufacturer who sent Him. We see again that to work is to become what you were born to be.

Thought: When you're deployed, you serve your natural gift to the world, and the world pays you for being yourself.

Reading: John 5:16–23

5. "Genesis 2:15," Interlinear Study Bible, StudyLight.org, https://www.studylight.org/interlinear-study-bible/greek/genesis/2-15.html.

—Day 38—
BECOMING RATHER THAN DOING

"For God's gifts and his call are irrevocable."

—Romans 11:29

Success does not come by *doing* something but by *becoming* something. That's why it's tough for people who decide that they want to become who they are and to grow the seed inside them. The traditional world has no room for them; it wants them to work for somebody else. But the world will have to *make room* for them.

You have to become yourself. Again, the future of your life is in your seed, or your gift. When you deploy yourself, you create your own environment and your own resources. You create your own revenue. And, once more, it starts with a change in thinking. You must understand that you're not a victim of your circumstances or the economic conditions of the day. Pay more attention to the Creator's laws and principles than you do to news reports about the economy.

Some people have multiple gifts, and that can make the process of finding their true work more difficult for them. The answer to this is to decide which gift you're going to focus on. You have to choose one and concentrate on it. You will be paid for what you master. Most people aren't looking for a generalist.

You have something no one else is able to offer. What you want to do is to be in a place where you can become who you really are and manifest your work. That's the goal. And your work can actually *become* your job if you are doing what you were born to do.

I also want to talk a little about retirement because the topic has significance for us in relation to becoming rather than doing. No matter what age you are, it's important to gain a new perspective about retirement. The idea of retirement is not in the Bible. It's a cultural concept. We are never supposed to "retire"; we are simply supposed to finish our work before we leave this earth. Please remember how we are defining *work*: becoming what we were born to be. If you stop becoming, you stop existing. Paul of Tarsus didn't retire before he died. But he did say, *"I have fought the good fight, I have finished the race, I have kept the faith"* (2 Timothy 4:7). We are to leave only after we finish something.

You might retire from your job, but you can't retire from your gift or your work. Often, people who live long lives are those who have found something they love to do throughout their life. Perhaps you have been retired for a few years and are beginning to scratch your head, saying, "Why did I retire?" I want to assure you that there's life after retirement, and you still have a future.

Ask God to show you the difference between your job and your work. I believe something good is going to happen to you when you discover your true work.

Thought: You might retire from your job, but you can't retire from your gift or your work.

Reading: 2 Timothy 4:6–8

—Day 39—

TRANSITIONING FROM YOUR JOB TO YOUR WORK

"I must be about My Father's business."

—Luke 2:49 (NKJV)

We often need to start out being employed at a job as we discover and deploy our true work. You don't have to leave your job right away. I want to show you how to make the most of where you are right now.

Jesus of Nazareth started out having a job. He was carpenter, following in the profession of His earthy father, Joseph. (See Matthew 13:55; Mark 6.) But His work was to redeem the human race—teaching us God the Father's laws and principles and restoring us to a relationship with Him. When Jesus was just twelve years old, He said, *"I must be about My Father's business"* (Luke 2:49 NKJV). He already knew what He was meant to do. Jesus also made statements such as these: "I work the works of Him who sent Me. My Father works; therefore I work. I came to complete the work My Father gave Me to do." (See John 4:34; 5:17; 10:37–38; 14:10.) Jesus was talking about His work, not His job. His work was to fulfill the purpose of the heavenly Father.

Thus, although our goal is deployment, employment can *prepare* us for deployment. Stay in your job as you develop your gift. Remember, you might even find your work in your job. Some people have found it there. For example, someone who was born to sing and who loves singing with a musical group in which they are paid to sing is not going to a job every day but is going to their work.

My advice is this: while you are at your job, learn as much as you can because, in my view, jobs are opportunities where you are paid to learn. Also, don't necessarily start out by trying to get a job that will only suit what you really like to do. And don't go for a job merely with the motivation of money. Instead, get a job that's available. Many people today don't want a job because they are waiting for one with the "right" salary. It isn't money that makes a job important. What makes a job significant is that you will be paid as you learn some new skills, have some new experiences, and meet some new people.

Sometimes you may be in a job not primarily for the purpose of being able to earn money but for building relationships. There are people with whom I used to work years ago, and my relationships with them have lasted, even though we've since gone our separate ways in terms of our work. These relationships have helped me in my life. Nurture relationships with the people around you—not for the purpose of "What can I get out of this person?" but for the enrichment of the relationships, which may bear mutual fruit and lead to open doors for you in the future.

Thought: Although our goal is deployment, employment can *prepare* us for deployment.

Reading: Luke 2:41–51 (NKJV, KJV)

—Day 40—

BEING "INDISPENSABLE"

"Humble yourselves before the Lord, and he will lift you up." —James 4:10

Those who know their purpose and understand the success within them will work at any job until it's time for their purpose to manifest. Remember that your job doesn't define you. You are bigger than the job you hold. Therefore, enjoy it for now. Why? You are just passing through that place. It's not your destiny. It's a temporary location for you to learn certain skills and perspectives, and you are paid to learn these things while you're on your way to greatness. This is why you should never despise a job, even as you realize it is temporary.

Learn all you can on your job. Perform that job well but don't depend on it. Begin to ignite your gift and create your work as you execute your job. Inside you is the wealthiest place in the world. As we've talked about, your gift is a seed that is currently ungerminated and unreleased but is full of potential.

While you are at employed at your job, although you can't fully depend on your position in terms of your financial security, you can actually make yourself so valuable to your company that you're the last one they will want to let go if there's an economic crunch. You can make yourself "indispensable" by enhancing the value you bring to your position.

How do you make yourself valuable as an employee? By refining your gift as you do your job and applying that gift in as many beneficial ways as possible while maintaining a positive attitude. Make yourself so important to the company by investing in your own gift that they won't want you to leave. You should read the book of Daniel in the Bible sometime. Daniel made himself so valuable that the king said he was an excellent worker, and no one could get rid of him.

If people in your company can't wait for you to leave, then you're not an asset and a help to them but a liability and a hindrance. You've made yourself a problem and a nuisance rather than a solution. When a downsizing takes place at a company due to a shortage in the cash flow, often, the first one to be let go is the one who causes all the problems.

As a matter of fact, the key to becoming prosperous is to *solve* problems. You are retained for the problems you solve. You are let go for the problems you create.

If you are seeking a job or want to improve your position at your company, look for a problem to solve. When you look for a problem and then solve that issue, you may be paid for it. If you make yourself indispensable to people by serving your gift with quality and becoming more and more valuable to them, they won't want to let you go. Use every job you have to refine your work.

Thought: The key to becoming prosperous is to solve problems.

Reading: Daniel 6:1–4

—Day 41—

BECOMING A PRODUCER

"Ship your grain across the sea; after many days you may receive a return." —Ecclesiastes 11:1

How do you go about developing your true work at the same time you're employed at your job? Cultivate the mindset of a producer and make valuable use of the time that is yours.

The most important statement I ever read in the Bible for setting me free from the idea of needing a job or of merely seeking employment is this one from wise King Solomon in Ecclesiastes: *"Ship your grain across the sea; after many days you may receive a return"* (Ecclesiastes 11:1). Solomon was discussing business. The phrase *"ship your grain across the sea"* refers to becoming an exporter, while the phrase *"receive a return"* refers to dividends. He was talking about getting a return on our investment. We're supposed to be producers and export what we produce. We need to think about ideas and inventions and stir them up inside us.

Solomon also said, *"Invest in seven ventures, yes, in eight; you do not know what disaster may come upon the land"* (verse 2). This is the same as saying, "Don't put all your eggs in one basket." We'll talk more about this in a later devotion when we discuss how to be successful in our domain. But here is a preview: Suppose someone is a barber who only cuts hair. They should actually go beyond cutting hair, in itself, in case their main business slows down for a time or they somehow become unable to use their skill. For instance, they might sell a line of hair products and other items that they have researched and found to be of good quality and for which there is a strong demand. If someone is a carpenter, they might diversify into supplying wood to builders or importing furniture. Such individuals would still be functioning within their gifts—styling, maintaining, and improving hair, and working with wood to create beautiful and functional items—while expanding the breadth and reach of the services and products they offer. These are just some simple examples to show you the possibilities of diversifying.

Solomon continued, "*Whoever watches the wind will not plant; whoever looks at the clouds will not reap*" (verse 4). The phrase "*whoever watches the wind*" refers to people who are waiting for ideal conditions or for luck. They hesitate to go out and work—and this means they won't ever reap. There may never be "ideal conditions," so we need to actively plant if we want to reap.

Thought: Cultivate the mindset of a producer and make valuable use of the time that is yours.

Reading: 2 Corinthians 9:6

—Day 42—

"SUCCESS AFTER 5:00"

> *"She sees that her trading is profitable, and her lamp does not go out at night."* —Proverbs 31:18

In yesterday's devotion, we began to explore Solomon's advice in Ecclesiastes 11 about being a producer and about diversifying. Solomon went on to say this:

> *Sow your seed in the morning, and at evening let your hands not be idle, for you do not know which will succeed, whether this or that, or whether both will do equally well.*
> (Ecclesiastes 11:6)

That is among the best advice I have ever heard. Here's the application: "Go to work in the morning, and when you get off from your job, keep working." Work on your skill during the day, and work on your gift afterward.

The hours between 8:00 a.m. and 5:00 p.m.—or whatever specific hours you work—belong to someone else's gift. This means that, although you should seek to apply your gift to your job, making yourself indispensable, you mainly grow in your gift on your own time. After hours, and when the weekend comes, that time fully belongs to your gift. So, give your employer your *skill* at 8:00 a.m., and release your *gift* at 5:00 p.m. This is a great key to success and prosperity.

I want to encourage you that what you're doing now isn't anything compared to what you could be doing! There's life after your job. I call it "Success after 5:00." Work persistently on developing your gift. My organization was built after 5:00 p.m. I had a day job at that time, and so did those who helped me to create the organization. We used to meet after finishing our jobs for the day, and we would work until two in the morning to establish it.

Many successful people began igniting their gift while others were sleeping. Of course, we all need a certain amount of rest, and people have different types of responsibilities to fulfill, but note what Solomon said in a proverb about "loving" sleep: *"Do not love sleep or you will grow poor; stay awake and you will have food to spare"* (Proverbs 20:13). Our culture says, "Go home and rest after work; you deserve it. Relax and watch TV." The Manufacturer's Manual says, "Let your hands not be idle." Those who are successful make that commitment because they have found something more important than a job.

Note the second part of this statement from Solomon from the earlier passage in Ecclesiastes: *"Sow your seed in the morning, and at evening let your hands not be idle,* ***for you do not know which will succeed, whether this or that, or whether both will do equally well.****"* You might have a job after your job or on the weekend, and both together can bring in a good sum. And you can actually work yourself out of a job. Your work can become so powerful that you don't need your job any longer.

Thought: Give your employer your *skill* at 8:00 a.m., and release your *gift* at 5:00 p.m.

Reading: Proverbs 31:10–31

—Day 43—

GIVE YOUR SEED THE RIGHT ENVIRONMENT

"Do not be misled: 'Bad company corrupts good character.'"
—1 Corinthians 15:33

You can have good "seed" with your gift and still be broke if your seed is not placed in the right environment. I mentioned earlier how, if you put a wheat seed on a tile floor and leave it there for twenty years, the wheat plant will remain in the seed. It's in the wrong environment for germination and growth. Similarly, if you're spending time with the wrong people, the wrong books, the wrong TV shows, and the wrong ideas, then you're placing yourself in the wrong environment for your seed to grow and bear fruit.

To me, friends are like fertilizer for my life and for my dreams. The wrong people in your life can be dream-killers. Just as your family members might not understand you, your friends and acquaintances might tell you that it's unrealistic for you to talk about having a dream, a vision, and a seed to sow. When they finish with you, you go right back to your old way of thinking. You have to give your mind and heart the right environment by spending time with people of vision and by reading, viewing, and thinking about things that will support the deployment of your gift.

Do you think you've been in a dry spell in your job for so long that there's nothing meaningful left for you to do in life? Have you responded to life's responsibilities by setting aside all your dreams? Do you think you're too old to cultivate your gift? Has anyone implied that your days of contributing to the world are over? Don't let discouragement or fatigue cause you to give up. What you need is the right environment—and you can cultivate the right environment for yourself to bring forth what's within your seed. Don't ever let anyone—not even yourself—write you off. Begin again to pursue your purpose. It will lead to your success.

I mentioned earlier that your work can become your job if you find your work *in* your job. You may drive every day or telecommute to a place of employment where you actually use your gift and are fulfilling your purpose. If you have a job where you are becoming who you are, then you are not "working a job"—you're "going to your work."

But if you have a job in which you cannot develop—or fully develop—your seed, you have to reach the point where your gift becomes more important to you than your job. When you see that there is life beyond your career, beyond your skill, you will enter into your true work, and you will become an agent of innovation and positive change in your generation.

Thought: Cultivate the right environment for yourself to bring forth what's within your seed.

Reading: 1 Peter 1:3–8

—Day 44—

FOUR STRATEGIES FOR SUCCESS IN YOUR DOMAIN

"But remember the Lord your God, for it is he who gives you the ability to produce wealth." —Deuteronomy 8:18

Over the next several devotions, we will focus on four principles of the Creator's purpose for our success and prosperity that we can apply to our unique domain of gifting. Let's begin by addressing how can we know that God wants us to be prosperous by looking at this example from the Manufacturer's Manual: *"You may say to yourself, 'My power and the strength of my hands have produced this wealth for me.' But remember the Lord your God, for it is he who gives you the ability to produce wealth, and so confirms his covenant, which he swore to your ancestors, as it is today"* (Deuteronomy 8:17–18).

First, the great leader Moses told the people whom he was leading, *"Remember the Lord your God, for it is he who gives you the ability to produce wealth."* This statement tells us *how* to become wealthy. Wealth doesn't come from God in the sense that He hands us money. Read it carefully. What does God give us? *"The* ***ability*** *to produce."* In previous devotions, we began to talk about becoming a producer as we develop our gift. We have been given an innate ability by the Creator to generate wealth. Consequently, wealth comes from finding our ability to produce something. When we produce, we either make something, work something out, or express something. Therefore, God gave us the skills, along with the laws, that, if put into practice, will result in prosperity.

Second, Moses told the people to be careful about how they thought about their prosperity: *"The Lord your God...is he who gives you the ability to produce wealth."* God is not against our becoming prosperous. He just wants us to remember and respect where that wealth came from and to use it wisely.

In Genesis, we find specific strategies for being a producer by using the seed that is within us. These strategies are at the heart of the process by which we express our true work to the world. Earlier, we saw how God said, *"Let Us make man in Our image, according to Our likeness"* (Genesis 1:26 NKJV). Shortly afterward, God said to the first human beings, *"Be fruitful and multiply; fill* [*"replenish"* KJV] *the earth and subdue it; have dominion over the fish of the sea, over the birds of the air, and over every living thing that moves on the earth"* (Genesis 1:28 NKJV).

Now, God is a good God. He knows those whom He has made, and He knows why He made them, so He tells them how to effect their purpose of dominion. Thus, this passage gives us the following essential instructions for success in exercising our inherent gifting: (1) *Be fruitful.* (2) *Multiply.* (3) *Fill,* or *replenish.* (4) *Subdue.*

To have dominion means to impact the environment with your gifting. You were born to *"have dominion over,"* or to "dominate," an area of life for which people will pay you, so that you can be personally fulfilled and financially prosperous. In tomorrow's devotion, we will begin to see how this transpires.

Thought: We have been given an innate ability by the Creator to generate wealth.

Reading: Proverbs 3:1–6

—DAY 45—
"THE LIFE-GIVING POWER OF GOD"

"Be fruitful and multiply; fill ["replenish" KJV*] the earth and subdue it."*
—Genesis 1:28

In God's instructions to the first human beings in Genesis 1:28, the verb *"be fruitful"* doesn't specifically refer to having children. Rather, it means to produce something. In Hebrew, it "expresses the idea of bringing forth, branching out, or yielding increase. In Scripture it is consistently tied to the life-giving power of God."[6]

The Creator didn't tell human beings to be "seedful." Why is that? He already assumed that we had seed within us—because He put it there. Instead, He told us to be *fruitful*. Your seed is already within you, and it has life in itself; you have the ability to produce the fruit by which you're supposed to prosper. What is fruit? It is "produce." When a tree produces fruit, it is evidence that what was inside the tree is now manifest.

Now, can one piece of fruit make us prosperous? No. God says, "Go to the next level: *multiply*." Suppose I had many crates filled with fruit sitting in a building on the grounds of my orchard. Would I be prosperous? No, I would have a lot of fruit, but I would still be broke if I didn't sell that fruit. So, even multiplying is not enough. We have to go to the third level: *replenish*.

Replenishing refers to distributing the product or service we have produced with our gift. But even if we distribute it, it might go to only a limited number of people, so we have to do something else in order to allow our gift to be prosperous. We have to move to the fourth level: *subdue*.

---

6. "6509. parah," Topical Lexicon, Bible Hub, https://biblehub.com/hebrew/6509.htm.

In this sense, the command to subdue means to control the market. What I mean by this is that when you start distributing your product or offering your service, it needs to become prominent in the marketplace so that, whenever people want that product or service, they will think of you.

At this point, I want to emphasize once more the following wise saying of Solomon: "*A man's gift makes room for him, and brings him before great men*" (Proverbs 18:16 NKJV). It doesn't say, "A man's education makes room for him." You may have a PhD and still be broke, because a PhD alone doesn't make you wealthy. Some people with PhDs have been hired by those who dropped out of school. Why? Because the person who doesn't have a PhD got an idea, and when they acted on that idea, it brought them prosperity. I am certainly a proponent of education, but it's not your education that brings you before great men—it's your gift.

That's why just attending a university doesn't make you successful. You don't go to a school to get your gift. Education can help to *refine* your gift, but it can't *give* it to you. Your gift was placed within you by the Manufacturer. So, allow your seed-gift to germinate and become fruitful so that it can be multiplied, distributed, and become prominent in the marketplace.

Thought: The Creator didn't tell human beings to be "seedful." Instead, He told us to be *fruitful*.

Reading: Genesis 49:22

—DAY 46—

SERVING YOUR GIFT

"Serve one another humbly in love." —Galatians 5:13

To better understand what I meant in yesterday's devotion about "subduing the market" with your gift, let's take a simple example of international fast-food restaurants. What are they especially known for? Their signature hamburgers. Can people buy one of those hamburgers at just any store? No. This is because the companies have refined their recipes; they use a specific system for making their hamburgers and their sauces. Similarly, you must refine your gift to make it distinct.

Yet creating those signature hamburgers, in themselves, didn't make these companies prosperous. They had to find a way to multiply them and their other products so that the same food was made according to the same system in every one of their restaurants. The companies trained their employees in how to make their burgers in order to maintain consistency. Then, in order to distribute their food to a wide number of customers, they established franchises.

The companies' franchises have now become so widespread that they have subdued the market for their particular signature hamburgers. Each fast-food restaurant has its own specialty items that draw their customers to select them over the others.

If you own a business or sell a product or service, do people make a point of going specifically to you for your goods or services to obtain what they want? Jesus of Nazareth said, *"Whoever wants to become great among you must be your servant, and whoever wants to be first must be your slave—just as the Son of Man did not come to be served, but to serve, and to give his life as a ransom for many"* (Matthew 20:26–28). If you want to be great, serve your gift to the world. If you want to be first, become a "slave" to your gift—work hard on developing it. In this context, being "first" means, again, being the first one people think of when they want what your product or service has to offer.

I receive invitations to speak from all over the world, and I sometimes ask myself, "Why are they inviting me, when there are many other people whom they might ask instead?" The answer is that I have developed a "signature product" that they feel they can't find anywhere else.

I have never invited myself to speak anywhere, whether it was at a corporation, a university, an organization, or a church. People came looking for the fruit I produced, and they invited me. I'm not teaching you something that I myself haven't done. I'm not different from you. But I was never taught this principle—I had to discover it on my own—and I want to pass it along because I desire the same results for you. I want to help you find your specialty item or service that will gain the attention of people in the marketplace so you can be successful. Produce fruit that people have to come to you for!

Thought: If you want to be great, serve your gift to the world.

Reading: Galatians 5:13–14

—Day 47—

BECOMING PEOPLE'S GO-TO

"Do to others what you would have them do to you, for this sums up the Law and the Prophets." —Matthew 7:12

The individual who becomes successful and prosperous is the one whom everybody wants or needs to go to in order to get something done. Why do you go to the dentist to have your teeth cleaned or to deal with a toothache? Because your dentist made themself valuable to you by learning to perform certain dental procedures that you need to have done but can't do for yourself. Why do you go to a doctor and give them your money, regardless of the state of the economy? Because your doctor made themself valuable to you by specializing in a field of knowledge through which they can address your medical needs. Why do you take your money to a lawyer? Because your lawyer made themself valuable to you by refining their gift to meet your legal needs.

If your car breaks down, your mechanic has the technical knowledge related to repairing it, so they tell you, "I'll fix it for five hundred dollars." You say, "Five hundred dollars?!" They reply, "I know the laws of car mechanics. If you want your car to work, it'll cost five hundred dollars." What's the difference between you and your mechanic? They have the knowledge and skill to fix your car, and you lack that knowledge and skill.

Here's a question to answer: Why should I come to you for your gift? How you answer that question tells me if you're going to be successful. The next question is even more difficult: Why should I give my money to you? What have you refined that would make me seek you out and pay for your product or service?

You have to realize that many people may already be doing something similar to what you're doing (or what you would like to be doing), so you can't do it in exactly the same way they do it. They have their own distinct way, so you each have a unique gift to offer. But just as a restaurant offers meals that people aren't able to imitate and therefore have to go to that specific restaurant to eat, find a way to make your product or service different from others'. When that product or service is unique and you are able to distribute it effectively, you will have "dominion."

As you begin to be fruitful and multiply your fruit, consider this: when a tree produces fruit, it is never for the tree itself. I've never seen a tree eat its own fruit, have you? Similarly, the seed within you that you were born with contains the potential for fruit, yet when that fruit is produced, it is not primarily intended for you but for others. However, you have to manifest that fruit so that others can see it and come to you for it. Trees don't bring their fruit to people. When a tree bears fruit, harvesters are attracted to it. The tree simply produces fruit, and the harvesters find the tree because they want what the tree has to offer. It is the fruit you produce that will attract and keep people's attention.

Thought: Why should others come to you for what your gift can offer them?

Reading: Matthew 7:7–12

— Day 48 —

"SUBDUING" THE MARKETPLACE, PART 1

"A woman from the city of Thyatira named Lydia [was] *a dealer in purple cloth."* —Acts 16:14

How can you more specifically apply the four strategies for exercising dominion? In this devotion, we will begin to look at some ways you can become successful in your domain and "subdue" the marketplace as you bear fruit through your gifting. These ways are applicable to both producing/distributing goods and offering services.

The first way is to give people added value or offer them something extra. There are many ways to add value to a customer's experience, whether it is with a specific type of product, a bonus item, a particular environment, or something else—so be creative! The effort will be worth it. Be sure to keep up the quality of your primary service while giving people this "something extra." If you are a chef who owns a restaurant, you might sell your specialty sauce to customers who want to take home a taste of your cooking. Or, suppose you sell shoes, and you currently offer a basic transaction of exchanging shoes for payment. You need to find a way to add value to your store. As you sell shoes, you might offer fresh hot coffee to every customer, providing a nice corner area in which they can sit and enjoy it. That's one small example of added value. If you take care in the preparation of the coffee, and the customers like it, they may pass the word: "When you go to that store, you'll get a great cup of coffee." You're creating an environment where people want to be.

We previously talked about making sure your product or service is distinct. There's something that you were born with that other people don't have in the way that you have it. So provide them with something no one else is able to give them, making it your specialty. Focus on a specific area of need that people have so that they'll come look for you. Suppose you are a beautician. Make your hairstyling services special. Perhaps obtain some extra training and study new techniques and styles, and then come back and tell people, "I'm the only one in our area who uses this technique and can offer these new hairstyles."

If you are a carpenter, focus on one area you enjoy doing, such as cabinets, and tell people, "I specialize in custom-made cabinets." That will make you stand out among other carpenters. If you just say you are a "carpenter," you will be compared to everyone else who is a carpenter. But if you are an expert at making custom cabinets, you have become valuable and significant because you have a refined gift. Or, suppose you want to open a restaurant. That can be a difficult business. People open restaurants all the time that close not long afterward. This is because many people don't just buy a sandwich; they buy a unique experience. Why should people come to your restaurant?

Whatever your domain of gifting, think about what you might offer that is unique and valuable.

Thought: Provide people with something no one else is able to give them, making it your specialty.

Reading: 1 Corinthians 12:4–7

—Day 49—

"SUBDUING" THE MARKETPLACE, PART 2

"Let each of you look out not only for his own interests, but also for the interests of others." —Philippians 2:4 (NKJV)

Today, we continue to look at ways in which you can "subdue" the marketplace, serving others with your gift. Sometimes quality alone is enough to enable you to stand out. Many customers want to make sure they are purchasing a product that is well made and will last, and they are willing to pay for it. What is the quality of your product or service? Is it sufficient to meet what your customers or potential customers are looking for?

Paying attention to detail is also good for business. For example, if you have a store, think about how to make your product displays more attractive. Discover what your customers like and find a way to personalize the product or service for them. If you play background music in your store, check to see if the style of music is what your customers want to hear while they are shopping. Make every aspect of the customer experience special and appealing. It will keep people coming.

Another way is to focus on good service. Don't try to cut corners or be careless in the way you interact with people. Let people know you care about them and about what they are looking to you to provide for them. When you offer true service, it's a whole new ball game for your business.

Additionally, finding out what people need will enable you to become a good business leader. People's needs can change over time. If someone comes to you and complains that you aren't doing something or aren't meeting a need, take that complaint seriously and consider its merit. You will always encounter individuals who complain just for the sake of it, yet some people may be expressing a real need that isn't being met but that you can remedy.

Finally, avoid focusing on a bottom line of trying to make money; instead, be genuinely interested in your clients or customers. If you do that, they'll be interested in you and what you have to offer.

Remember that you were born to solve a problem. That's where ideas for businesses come from. A business is simply a way of solving people's problems or meeting their needs. Potential businesses are all around us because problems are all around us. When I first saw a massage chair at an airport, it was in Asia. I thought, "Something has started here." Now, almost every airport seems to offer massage chairs. Why? Because people find their muscles getting tight when they travel, and they need to relax. Someone recognized that problem and thought, "I can solve this," and they turned it into a lucrative business.

So, as you think about your gift, think about problems that need to be solved and how your gift ties into a solution to them. Study the problems around you and in the world. You'll be amazed at what you see. At the same time, listen for complaints, because every complaint is also a potential business. You were given the ability to solve a problem, and I believe that anyone who solves problems can become prosperous.

Thought: Let people know you care about them and about what they are looking to you to provide for them.

Reading: Philippians 2:1–4

—Day 50—

RESPONDING TO CHALLENGING TIMES

"In all things God works for the good of those who love him, who have been called according to his purpose."

—Romans 8:28

How do we respond to challenging times—when life hits us on the blind side and we didn't expect things to go the way they did, when everything seems to be crumbling around us—so that we can keep moving forward on our journey of success? Perhaps you have experienced one of these scenarios or something like it:

- You feel like the system has spat you out with no regard for you as an individual.
- There's not enough money at the end of each month to take care of your financial obligations.
- You've completely lost your source of income, your house, your car—and it feels like you've lost your sanity too.
- Your company has shut down or your business has gone under.

A crisis is a situation or an event that affects us and our environment and by which we are victimized. In the natural world, we consider a hurricane, a tornado, a tsunami, or a blizzard to be a crisis because it is a circumstance that we did not cause and over which we have no direct control. In the same way, we face crises in our life that we did not cause and cannot directly control. Put simply, a crisis is an unplanned and uncontrollable change.

There are times when we may generate a crisis for ourselves. Perhaps we mismanaged our funds, buying things that we couldn't afford and didn't need. We spent more money than we brought in, and now we are deeply in debt: that is a natural consequence that is built into our violation of a financial law. But if we lost our job because our company laid us off, we can't control that. If the number of clients in our business has suddenly dropped, so that we can't make enough money to keep things going, and we have to shut down, that's an unplanned change. Whatever the nature or origin of a crisis, it attacks our equilibrium. Over the next few days, we will talk about how we can respond to this.

Note that during difficult times or crisis periods, you may have to take a job just so that you can survive. That is not a season to hold on to your pride, pretending that everything thing is all right and not doing anything about your financial situation to the point that your children go hungry. There are times when you have to get a job until you can get your work back.

No matter what you're facing, don't allow yourself to panic for too long. You may panic for a minute! But then let the panicking time be over because whatever difficult situation you're in, you're going to come out of it.

Thought: There are times when you have to get a job until you can get your work back.

Reading: Romans 8:26–27

—Day 51—
"TO EVERYTHING THERE IS A SEASON"

"To everything there is a season, a time for every purpose under heaven." —Ecclesiastes 3:1 (NKJV)

Nothing is permanent except for God, His laws, and His promises. Everything else changes. As a matter of fact, God promises us that nothing will remain the same: *"To everything there is* [only] *a season, a time for every purpose under heaven"* (Ecclesiastes 3:1 NKJV). Therefore, everything that you experience is only seasonal.

If you're broke now, it's only a seasonal insolvency. You're only passing through a tough moment. You're going to move into a time of prosperity. If your company closed, if your business failed, then give it a good funeral and bury it, but then be prepared for a resurrection. You'll be back, because everything is only for a season.

The principle that there is a season for everything is one of the most important principles I have learned in life. It has helped me to understand that we are running a race, and our success is a process rather than an end. If one part of our life has ended or changed, that is not the end of our purpose or success. In times of difficulty and crisis, we need to remember that success has more to do with moving in the right direction than coming to a destination.

In such times, we need to stop waiting for the economy to turn around or for the government to institute an economic policy. We have our own kingdom "governmental policies," and they work every time. We can turn the economy around in our own life. There's no lack of money in the world. Wealth follows laws—it doesn't follow mere wishes. Your gift cannot be a victim of the economy, and a crisis cannot destroy it. Instead, the crisis you are experiencing may manifest your gift.

Laws have no crises. Whether you are experiencing good times or difficult ones, I want you to recognize that God has built certain laws into His systems and products—including you—that guarantee their function, in order to protect His reputation, confirming that what He has made is good and functions well. Imagine a lighthouse with a wave breaking against it: the wave is moving, but the lighthouse remains grounded. God's laws are like a lighthouse—they never move. And like anything that has to do with success in life, coming out of a crisis is 100 percent law-based.

It doesn't matter what the issues in our life are or what the culture is doing; if we know laws and principles, we will overcome our circumstances. We must live by those laws and principles rather than by our feelings. Of course, we have feelings, but we are not guided by those feelings when challenges arise.

Whatever you are facing, you can say to God, "Deliver me for Your name's sake. Do it for Your own reputation." When I have a need, I say, "Lord, this isn't good for You. I will tell everybody how You provided for me." My needs keep being met. That's what I meant when I wrote earlier about "putting pressure" on God because our success is good for our Creator.

Thought: Success has more to do with moving in the right direction than coming to a destination.

Reading: Genesis 8:22

—Day 52—

TESTS CREATE CREDIBILITY

"The testing of your faith produces perseverance."

—James 1:3

Challenging times may come to us just because we are exercising our gift. Please keep in mind that all gifts will be tested for authenticity. When you decide to stop being an employed person and become a deployed person, all your "enemies" will wake up. You have to be ready for the fight and stay focused. The testing comes to prove your dedication and commitment to your gift. Yet a vision that has been tested will eventually be trusted. When I began working on my dream, none of my family members understood me. But they all ended up supporting me, and some have come to work for me.

Perhaps your vision is being tested right now. You find it difficult to do what you're doing because nobody else is doing it. You wonder why it's so hard. You're working a job at the same time that you're working on your dream because you know you *have* to keep working on that dream. While there will be tests, let me tell you the good news: the tests don't come to destroy your gift—they come to prove your gift. Stay with it!

Whatever test you are undergoing now will create credibility for your life and will build trust in other people toward you. If you're experiencing a financial crisis, that's a test to see if you can be trusted on the other side of the crisis. Never think that a crisis comes to end your life. It comes to give trustworthiness to it. The resilience you show and the constructive responses you manifest in the midst of your troubles will earn you the respect of those who are observing you during that trial.

This brings us back to one of the laws we talked about earlier: you don't trust a product that hasn't been tested. People are looking for those who are unafraid to bring out their gift and to persevere with the plans they believe in, even—or especially—in the midst of difficulty. My organization used to be called a fly-by-night phenomenon that wouldn't last, but we survived that criticism. You are never trusted for the things you claim. You are always trusted for the things you have survived.

Some people will hope that you fail, and then, when you make it, they will congratulate you! Consequently, don't listen to the naysayers. Accept the test as part of your becoming a successful person. Successful people always have survival testimonies. They weren't born successful. Success comes to people as a result of their having survived being criticized and attacked, of their having survived the test of the fiery furnace of life, knowing that God is always with them (see Daniel 3), of their having survived being thrown into a pit with lions (see Daniel 6). Success is what people think of you *after* they try to kill you!

So, I encourage you to get ready for the test. Sometimes, you will never be completely accepted until you've first been completely rejected. People will trust you for what you have survived.

Thought: The tests don't come to destroy your gift—they come to prove your gift.

Reading: James 1:2–4

—Day 53—

BENEFITS OF A CRISIS, PART 1

"Be transformed by the renewing of your mind."

—Romans 12:2

Besides winning us credibility, there are other benefits that can come as a result of a crisis that enable us to fulfill our purpose in life. I love this statement by Shakespeare, the great playwright: "Sweet are the uses of adversity."[7] That's a deep statement. Shakespeare caught on to something. He realized that adversity can benefit the one experiencing the hardship. He was telling us that when things are adverse, when things are in crisis, we can use them to attain a positive outcome. Everything that happens to you can be used to produce something good.

Over the next few days, we will explore principles of crisis that will lead us to success and prosperity in the midst of difficulty. Some of these areas interact or overlap with one another, yet each addresses a distinct outcome from which we can profit.

First, a crisis is the incubator of creativity. Most of the time, we don't think in creative ways and in new patterns until something negative happens to us. When things fall apart, it makes us think outside the box. A crisis demands innovative thinking. It makes us think about things in ways we have never thought about them before. Consider this: after God created Adam, He didn't give him a finished table or a chair. He gave Adam (and his descendants) trees, in which tables and chairs were "hidden," and He essentially said, "Work with that."

---

7. William Shakespeare, *As You Like It*, ed. Agnes Latham (London: The Arden Shakespeare, 2005), 2.2.12. References are to act, scene, and line.

When has a crisis forced you to think about something in a fresh way? How could thinking creatively help you with a current difficulty in your life?

Second, a crisis demands a new way of thinking about old problems. Here is what I mean: Suppose you have a long-standing need to pay your mortgage each month. If you are laid off or fired from your job, the issue is that the source of income with which you used to pay your mortgage has dried up—but the old problem hasn't gone away. You still have to pay installments on your mortgage. You are therefore compelled to think in a new way in order to figure out how you can generate income to pay for the old problem.

What "old problem" do you currently have to approach in a new way? How can you find alternate means to address it?

Third, crisis ignites a passion for a renewed vision. Sometimes we stray from our purpose, and God has to pull the rug out from under us to get us back on track. Often, a crisis will make us stop and reflect on the original idea that the Creator revealed to us. It will prompt us to return to our true passion and vision.

Are you on track with your purpose and gift? If not, how will you actively return to being on track?

Thought: "Sweet are the uses of adversity."

Reading: Romans 12:1–2

—Day 54—
BENEFITS OF A CRISIS, PART 2

"Do not dwell on the past." —Isaiah 43:18

A crisis pushes us to grow and improve ourselves. Sometimes, we become stuck in one place for too long, and the only way for us to get where we need to be is for something to happen that pushes us to a new place. We often don't grow until we are stretched to do so. Thus, a crisis can result in our making an effort to improve ourselves in some way and to activate more of our potential than we otherwise would have.

The problem with human beings is that we are creatures of habit. We need to break patterns that hold us back. For example, we may have a habit of being broke all the time. Even when we do have money, we end up spending it just to make sure we are broke again because being without money feels familiar to us. If we experience an extreme financial crisis in our life, that pattern can be interrupted because we come to a place where we and our family members need to survive, and we start implementing sound financial principles to get through the emergency. The experience shows us the benefits of following those principles consistently in our lives.

If you are currently facing a crisis, what occasions for personal growth and the creation of new patterns do you see?

A crisis can also challenge our experience. It has a way of shaking loose areas of our life that we thought would always stay the same. When a crisis comes, some of your past experiences, skills, and ways of doing thing may become useless. What do you do when things you previously knew and depended on are no longer working for you? Experience can sometimes be your worst enemy if you have been doing something in a certain way but the environment has changed and your previous know-how is no longer relevant or needed. If you are going through something like this, you may have to retool yourself, relearn some things, or gain new skills. Perhaps you have never performed a certain job before, but it has become necessary for you to learn how to do it in order to support yourself or to move forward in your purpose. Will you accept that challenge?

Someone who needs to support themself and their family might say, "I can't do that job. It's below me." We can come out of anything, but if we idly sit at home, we aren't activating the laws that can make us prosperous. So, if we were laid off, and a job opens up, we can say to ourselves, "I'm going to take it for a season." Then, we can apply the principle of "Success after 5:00" to develop our true work again.

Has your environment changed so that some of your past experiences or skills are no longer relevant, and your holding on to them is keeping you from success? In what ways could you retool yourself in this new environment?

Thought: We often don't grow until we are stretched to do so.

Reading: Isaiah 43:18–19

—Day 55—

BENEFITS OF A CRISIS, PART 3

"Faith is confidence in what we hope for and assurance about what we do not see." —Hebrews 11:1

A crisis can be the catalyst of development. Jon Huntsman Sr. wrote, "If there is a silver lining to bad times, it is this: When facing severe challenges, your mind normally is at its sharpest. Humans have seldom created anything of lasting value unless they were tried or hurting."[8]

Let's talk about two statements within this quote. First, Huntsman said that when you are experiencing the biggest trials, this is when your mind is normally at its sharpest. Your mind is in crisis mode and has to think of things it has never thought of before. Second, he said, "Humans seldom have created anything of lasting value unless they were tried or hurting." He was speaking from experience, saying that we don't produce anything of note unless we are under pressure.

Therefore, when we face a crisis, it forces us to develop new approaches to life and to the process of living. Probably every progressive invention came out of a problem. That's because a crisis makes us imagine unique approaches, and this leads to our developing solutions and innovative ways of doing things. What is something beneficial that you could develop or produce in response to the pressure you are experiencing?

With new ways of doing things and new inventions come new opportunities, industries, fields of endeavor, and reforms. What opportunities for progress do you recognize in your life and in the

8. Jon M. Huntsman, *Winners Never Cheat: Even in Difficult Times* (Upper Saddle River, NJ: Pearson Education, Inc., 2014), 6.

world around you? What new industries and activities do you see in your community and nation that fit your gifting?

A crisis also manifests true leadership ability. No matter how much someone might claim to be a leader, only when they experience a challenging time can they *prove* that they are a leader. You are not really a leader in good times. While everyone has leadership potential within them, genuine leadership is tested and verified in a crisis environment.

A crisis tests whether we are as mature as we claim to be. Perhaps we've been telling people how good God has been to us. Do we still make the same claim when things fall apart in our lives? Or perhaps we've been expressing to others how much faith we have. Let's see what kind of faith we have when we are in a situation where things don't look very good and we wonder how we're going to make it to the next day. How do your leadership ability and principles hold up when you are under pressure?

Think about all the benefits of crisis that we have reviewed over the past several days, and ask God to help you to begin creating benefits out of the difficult period you are going through.

Thought: A crisis makes us imagine unique approaches, and this leads to our developing solutions and innovative ways of doing things.

Reading: Philippians 4:12–13

—Day 56—

BACK TO THE BASICS

"The generous will themselves be blessed, for they share their food with the poor." —Proverbs 22:9

If you are experiencing any form of challenge or crisis, consider carefully how you might glean from it lessons and opportunities that can benefit you. At the same time, focus on some of the basics in life that will sustain you. Among those basics are the practices of generosity and thankfulness. Sometimes we make things complicated and try to work things out and calculate what we need to do next when the best thing we can do is to look away from our problems for the moment and look toward helping other people.

Solomon wrote, "*The generous will themselves be blessed, for they share their food with the poor.*" And Jesus taught, "*Give, and it will be given to you. A good measure, pressed down, shaken together and running over, will be poured into your lap. For with the measure you use, it will be measured to you*" (Luke 6:38). If you are having financial difficulty, you might not have much money to give away, but what else might you give to someone? It could be as simple as offering your time and your tools to a neighbor's building project, donating canned food from your own pantry to a food drive, or baking someone a cake.

There might be other things that you can share with others as well. For example, perhaps you use your car mainly to drive to work. Why not put it to use serving people, such as giving an older person a ride to the grocery store or to a doctor's appointment? By doing this, you will be activating a law: "*Give, and it will be given to you.*"

Thousands of years ago, one of the psalmists wrote this timeless truth: *"Give thanks to the Lord, for he is good; his love endures forever"* (Psalm 106:1). You can give God thanks for what He will do to show you your purpose and to bring you out of your difficulties for His name's sake. God has said, *"I know the plans I have for you,...plans to prosper you and not to harm you, plans to give you hope and a future"* (Jeremiah 29:11). He says He has a plan to give us hope, so He has to make sure we reach the fruit-bearing stage. He has to make sure we fulfill our destiny because His name is on the line. He's going to fix things because of His reputation. Hope is coming.

Let's remember that Matthew, one of Jesus's disciples, reported Jesus as saying, *"Seek first his kingdom and his righteousness, and all these things will be given to you as well"* (Matthew 6:33). Seek first the kingdom of God, and these things will be what? *"Given to you as well."* What *"things"*? The answer is whatever provision you need to live and to fulfill your purpose—in times of peace and in times of crisis—leading to your success.

Thought: Sometimes the best thing we can do is to look away from our problems for the moment and look toward helping other people.

Reading: Psalm 100

—Day 57—

TEN KEYS FOR PERSONAL SUCCESS: #1 PURPOSE AND #2 PERCEPTION

"And who knows but that you have come to your royal position for such a time as this?" —Esther 4:14

I have found it helpful to encapsulate many of the concepts and principles I teach about success into "Ten Keys for Personal Success" so that they can stay in the forefront of our mind and we can be daily reminded to put them into practice. These keys both reinforce and expand on themes we have discussed so far. The ten keys are *purpose, perception, potential, passion, principles, plan, people, persistence, perseverance,* and *prayer.* All ten keys start with the letter *p* so that we can more easily remember them. In today's devotion, we will cover the first two keys.

I can't emphasize enough that, to be successful, you *must* start by having a personal sense of purpose—an awareness of the reason for your existence. We have seen that our purpose is the original intent of the Manufacturer—the God of creation—for us. Without a clear idea of your purpose, you can't start the process of success because success means accomplishing the purpose you were put on earth to fulfill. The seed of our success is hidden in our purpose and in the gift we have been given to carry out that purpose. If you haven't yet begun to actively seek out your purpose and the specific contribution you were destined to make to your generation, I urge you to begin doing so today.

The second key, perception, is based on the principle that you can't follow a path that you can't see. I like to say that having perception, or vision, is "seeing your purpose in pictures"—in other words, having a clear conception of where you are going.

God gave humanity the gift of perception so that we would not have to live only by what we see but would also have the ability to imagine what *can be* and to make it a reality. We know that our purpose is already "finished" and that God has placed within us the potential for fulfilling it. And we see our purpose through faith. To paraphrase the writer of the book of Hebrews, faith is the substance of things you hope to accomplish, the evidence of things you can see even when others cannot. (See Hebrews 11:1 NKJV, KJV.) When you don't have a vision for your future and destiny, you will likely relive the past with its disappointments and failures. Only by seeing what is not yet here can you bring something new, creative, and exciting into existence.

Everything we do—the way we conduct our entire life—should be guided by our perception of the purpose God has placed in our heart. It must influence what we spend our time and money on and what our priorities are.

Thus, it doesn't matter what you currently have or don't have, as long as you can see what you *could* have. Perception is a key to success because where there's a dream, there's hope, and where there's hope, there's faith.

Thought: Without perception, our life will have no sense of direction, our activities will have no meaning, our time will have no purpose, and our resources will have no application.

Reading: Jeremiah 33:3

—Day 58—

TEN KEYS FOR PERSONAL SUCCESS: #3 POTENTIAL AND #4 PASSION

"For we live by faith, not by sight." —2 Corinthians 5:7

In today's devotion, we will explore the next two keys for personal success: *potential* and *passion*.

Your potential is directly related to your perception, in which you imagine what can be. You must believe in your innate potential to reach the fulfillment of your dream more than other people's assessment of you or what the "odds" look like.

Potential is hidden capacity, untapped power, unreleased energy. It is all that you could be but haven't yet become. It is who you really are, even if you don't yet know your true self. You must come into an awareness of this capacity within you.

Whatever you were born to do, you are equipped to do. Moreover, resources will become available to you as you need them. Whatever God is calling you to dream is a revelation of your ability. What this means is that God gives ability to fulfill responsibility. God would never give you an assignment without also granting you the facility to undertake it and the provision for it—either now or at a later time when it is needed. Therefore, when you begin to move forward with your dream, you will uncover your ability and your provision. God has created you to do something wonderful, and you have genuine potential to fulfill that purpose.

Passion is also birthed from perception—from a revelation of where you are headed in life. Every great man or woman became great because they possessed the spirit of passion. Yet I believe that the majority of the people in the world lack true passion for living. I think that passion is rare in human experience.

Passion may be defined in various ways, including the following:

A deep desire. Passion is stamina that says, "I'm going to go after this, no matter what happens. If I have to wait five, ten, or fifteen years, I will get it." If you want to go all the way to your dream, you can't sit back and expect everything to be easy.

An intense commitment. Many people are interested in doing certain things, but they aren't really committed to doing them. Those who are successful are willing to put their whole self into accomplishing their dream. Passionate people are those who have discovered something more important than life itself.

A clear motivation. Passion is the juice for living. Having a clear motivation in life helps us to rise above our daily routine. Do you have an inner motivation to follow your dream?

When the Creator's purpose for you is so vivid that you can see it in your mind's eye, then that mental picture will create within you an enthusiasm to fulfill it. It will ignite within you a deep desire to make your unique contribution to this world. You know that you have tapped into your potential for success when you are so actively involved in the things you want to do that you can't stop thinking about them and working on them.

Thought: It is only when we have a passion for what we desire to do that things start happening to enable us to fulfill it. Passion ignites results.

Reading: Ephesians 3:20–21

—DAY 59—

TEN KEYS FOR PERSONAL SUCCESS: #5 PRINCIPLES

"I will walk about in freedom, for I have sought out your precepts." —Psalm 119:45

Earlier in this devotional, we explored the origin and nature of the Manufacturer's laws and principles—and our essential need to align our life with them in our journey of success. The fifth key for personal success is therefore *principles*.

After the Manufacturer created human beings, He gave them valuable information about how they functioned, how to properly operate their life, and how to ensure that they would be successful. Later on in human history, He made sure that these principles, as well as additional instructions, were put into writing as a vital reference for all of humanity. The laws and principles contained in the biblical record are time-tested and stable. When we follow these laws and principles, we protect and preserve our vision and passion.

Following spiritual laws will lead us to success in practical matters—such as the best way to handle finances, business matters, and relationships—as well as in moral ones. Spiritual laws enable us to know how to respond in constructive ways to real-world challenges related to exercising our gift and also to ethical issues that we will inevitably face along the way. For example, in one section of the Manufacturer's Manual, Jesus of Nazareth discussed our need to address our own shortcomings before trying to correct others' faults:

Why do you look at the speck of sawdust in your brother's eye and pay no attention to the plank in your own eye? How can you say to your brother, "Brother, let me take the speck out of your eye," when you yourself fail to see the plank in your own eye? You hypocrite, first take the plank out of your eye, and then you will see clearly to remove the speck from your brother's eye. (Luke 6:41–42)

Perhaps you are building a business or providing a service, but you have been ignoring time-honored principles from the Manufacturer. The growth of a business or service is not all about strategic business plans, astute investments, and talented employees. You also have to conduct your business or other work honestly, make wise decisions, and hire people with integrity—those who have a passion for the corporate vision and who value and support the contributions of all their coworkers.

Committing—or recommitting—to the Creator's laws and principles is like rebooting a stalled computer by pushing the reset button: it allows us to return to the "original mode" where we can function as we were intended to. By studying and implementing these principles, you will avoid moral compromise and ethical missteps. You will protect yourself from the negative effects that such mistakes inevitably have on other aspects of your life, including the exercise of your gifts and the realization of your potential. We will talk further in coming devotions about how to establish an ethical foundation for our life as the underpinning for success, discussing how we can determine and write out the core principles by which we will live and conduct ourselves.

Thought: When we follow God's laws and principles, we protect and preserve our vision and passion.

Reading: Psalm 119:159–160

—Day 60—

TEN KEYS FOR PERSONAL SUCCESS: #6 PLAN, PART 1

"To humans belong the plans of the heart, but from the Lord comes the proper answer of the tongue." —Proverbs 16:1

When you apply to your life the ten essential keys we are looking at, they will all work together to create a fruitful atmosphere and a secure framework that will enable you to succeed. Each key is significant and distinct, and supports the others. Let us now consider the next key: *plan*.

Those who are successful develop a clear plan for what they desire to do. I've known people who have tried to be successful over and over again without having a plan. It doesn't work.

I'm a stickler for planning. Anyone who works with me will tell you that. One of the reasons I continually emphasize that we need to know and focus on our purpose is because plans that don't help us fulfill our purpose are counterproductive to our life. But if we follow a plan based on our purpose, then that plan can unfold, and what we desire to do can become a reality.

Solomon wrote, *"To humans belong the plans of the heart, but from the Lord comes the proper answer of the tongue."* That's a very powerful statement. God is saying, in effect, "I gave you your purpose and gift, as well as the perception to see your purpose in pictures. Now, you put the plan on paper, and I will work out the details." If we don't have a plan, how can God direct us?

Do you know what you want to do next week, next month, next year, five years from now? Do you have a plan for the next twenty years of your life? God has given you the ability to do that. He has given you a mind, the gift of imagination, and the vision of faith. Your dream is worth fleshing out and writing down. If God gave you the dream, it deserves to be done. God says He will explain how your plan will be accomplished, yet He can't discuss it with you until you have something concrete to talk about.

Ask yourself what practical steps you need to take to reach your dream. You must answer and take action on questions such as the following for the success of your plan:

1. What do I want to accomplish?
2. Who do I need?
3. What do I have?
4. Where can I go for information?
5. What should I read?
6. What courses or what type of education might be helpful or necessary?
7. With whom should I associate?
8. How long should it take?
9. How much will it cost?
10. Where can I get experience?

You may need to adjust or refine the specifics of your plan as God leads you through the process of its fulfillment, but you first need to identify and clarify where you are headed so that you can begin. Have you made a plan for where God is leading you to go in life?

Thought: What practical steps do you need to take to reach your dream?

Reading: Proverbs 16:9

—Day 61—

TEN KEYS FOR PERSONAL SUCCESS: #6 PLAN, PART 2

> *"Won't you first sit down and estimate the cost to see if you have enough money to complete it?"* —Luke 14:28

Jesus said that a wise person doesn't start to build something unless they first work out the details. (See Luke 14:28–30.) In this devotion, we continue to examine the sixth key for personal success: making a *plan*. You may need to adjust or refine the specifics of your plan as God leads you through the process of its fulfillment, but you first need to identify and clarify where you are headed so that you can begin. As you go through the process, you can do the following to cultivate your plan: (1) identify, (2) clarify, (3) refine, (4) document, (5) articulate, (6) communicate, (7) demonstrate, (8) reevaluate, (9) revise, and (10) repeat.

Besides having a general plan, you need to set goals and objectives so that you can be ready to carry out your plan. A goal may be defined as an established point of achievement that leads to a greater accomplishment, a point of measure for progress toward an ultimate purpose, or a prerequisite for the achievement of an ultimate plan.

Success comes from the discipline of setting goals according to your purpose. Goals give us a structure for completing our plan one step at a time. They give us a starting place and an ending place, and they help us to focus. Where you end up in life is a result of the goals that you set or do not set. If you don't have any goals for yourself, other people will run your life. And the more successful you become, the more people will compete for your time, so you have to guard your goals even more carefully then. Those who are successful are always zealous for and jealous of their goals because these goals represent their lives. When our goals change, our lives change.

After you establish your goals, you should write out your objectives, which are a detailed breakdown of your goals. They determine when you want things to happen. You must clearly delineate what you need to do and when you need to do it in order to get to where you want to go. Objectives should include specific timetables.

To fulfill your plan, it is necessary not only to discipline yourself to follow your goals and objectives but also to seek wise counsel. At any stage of life, it is a good practice for us to seek the counsel of two or three people whom we trust before making a major decision, carefully listening to and weighing their answers according to our personal vision and values. Solomon wrote, *"Plans fail for lack of counsel, but with many advisers they succeed"* (Proverbs 15:22).

Thought: Success comes from the discipline of setting goals according to your purpose.

Reading: Luke 14:28–30

—Day 62—

TEN KEYS FOR PERSONAL SUCCESS: #7 PEOPLE

"So that I may come to you with joy, by God's will, and in your company be refreshed." —Romans 15:32

The seventh key to personal success, *people,* refers to the fact that you must guard yourself from the wrong people while gathering around yourself the right people.

Having the right people in your life means being around those who will support you in your goals—those who will partner with you and influence you to reach them. In contrast, having the wrong people around you is dangerous because they will pull you away from your purpose and from success.

When thinking about the people in your life, consider the law of association. This law states that *you become like those with whom you spend time.* People have the potential to create your environment. Your environment then determines your mindset, and your mindset determines your future. Thus, you must choose your friends and associates judiciously, selecting those who are truly with you and not against you. Ask yourself, "With whom am I spending time?" and "What effect are these people having on me and on my purpose?"

In addressing the consequences that come with the law of association, I have had to learn to take the following three actions to protect my purpose:

1. *Disassociation.* There are people and places that you are going to have to disassociate yourself from if you're going to make it to your dream. Don't be afraid to disassociate yourself from people who aren't right for you. Disassociation

doesn't have to be confrontational. Sometimes, you can ease out of someone's life very quietly, just as you eased into it. Disassociation is not an easy action to take, but it is a very important priority in life.

2. *Limited association.* You may not want to completely disassociate yourself from some of the people in your life. However, it is important that you thoughtfully determine how much time you will spend with them.
3. *Expanded association.* You protect your mental environment by spending major time with positive influences and minor time with negative influences. Therefore, to be successful, you need to increase the time you spend with people who have the same philosophy, goals, and discipline that you do, people who exhibit the kind of character and vision that you desire to have.

Key 7 also has this component: God has people prepared to work with you, and they will be of great benefit to you. Although we each receive a personal purpose and gift, we were not created to fulfill our vision by ourselves. Our gift will attract others who will contribute toward the completion of our dream. It is not God's method to give a particular assignment or vision to a group. He gives a unique vision to an individual who then shares their vision with the group and transfers it to them. The members of the group then run with the vision because they find in it a place for their own personal vision to be fulfilled. This is how God weaves personal and corporate vision together.

Thought: You become like those with whom you spend time.

Reading: Romans 15:23–24

—Day 63—

TEN KEYS FOR PERSONAL SUCCESS: #8 PERSISTENCE

"Ask and it will be given to you; seek and you will find; knock and the door will be opened to you." —Luke 11:9

In the "Ten Keys for Personal Success," I have included the quality of *persistence* because we will inevitably encounter various forms of resistance as we move toward accomplishing our purpose.

One reason we need persistence in our journey of success is that there will be those who don't believe in us or what we are doing. We must get used to that reality. It's part of the process of attaining success. This means that you will have to fight to achieve your dream. Dreams don't come to you—you go for them. Like potential and passion, persistence springs from perception, or vision. Once you know what you really want and can "see" it, then, no matter what comes against you, you never give up. Persistence may be defined as:

- The ability to face defeat again and again and not give up
- The knack for pushing on in the face of difficulty, knowing that victory is yours
- The determination to work hard at overcoming every obstacle and to do whatever is necessary to reach your goals

When we are persistent, this is a manifestation that we hold a strong conviction about our future based on the purpose God has given us for our life. We feel that the attainment of our purpose is not optional but is an obligation and a necessity, so we would never think of abandoning our goal. Jesus told a parable that encourages us in that it shows how success comes to those who persist—not only in the natural realm but also in the spiritual realm:

> *Suppose you have a friend, and you go to him at midnight and say, "Friend, lend me three loaves of bread; a friend of mine on a journey has come to me, and I have no food to offer him." And suppose the one inside answers, "Don't bother me. The door is already locked, and my children and I are in bed. I can't get up and give you anything." I tell you, even though he will not get up and give you the bread because of friendship, yet because of your shameless audacity he will surely get up and give you as much as you need. So I say to you: Ask and it will be given to you; seek and you will find; knock and the door will be opened to you. For everyone who asks receives; the one who seeks finds; and to the one who knocks, the door will be opened.* (Luke 11:5–10)

Thus, as long as a person can hold on to their vision, there is always a chance for them to move out of their present circumstances and toward the fulfillment of their purpose. When you know your purpose in pictures, you know how to stay in the race and complete it.

Thought: Once you know what you really want and can "see" it, then, no matter what comes against you, you never give up.

Reading: Galatians 6:9

—Day 64—

TEN KEYS FOR PERSONAL SUCCESS: #9 PERSEVERANCE

"[God] *gives strength to the weary and increases the power of the weak.*" —Isaiah 40:29

Persistence and perseverance are related: one definition of *persevere* is "to persist in a state, enterprise, or undertaking in spite of counterinfluences, opposition, or discouragement."[9] However, each of these qualities makes a distinct contribution to our success.

While being persistent generally means to keep pushing forward, persevering essentially means to bear up under pressure. Perseverance is the power to endure, to hold on, in spite of everything. Again, when you begin to act on your gifting, it will stir up both those who want to help you and those who want to hinder you. Opposition is often proof that you're really doing something with your life.

Although, as you pursue your purpose, you may continue to get knocked down, when you persevere, you get up again each time and dust yourself off, saying, "I'm going to start again. I'm going to try one more time—two more times, ten more times." In the 2012 Olympics held in London, there were four young Bahamian men who ran the men's 4x400 relay race and won the gold medal. This was the first Olympic men's gold medal in any sport for the Bahamas. Most people watching the Olympics only saw these four young athletes compete on television. They never witnessed their training habits or knew their history. The oldest one among them,

9. Merriam-Webster.com Dictionary, s.v. "persevere," https://www.merriam-webster.com/dictionary/persevere.

Chris Brown, had tried and failed to win a gold medal many times, but he kept coming back and finally reached his dream.[10]

What about you? Do you keep coming back when life gets difficult? William Feather said, "Success seems to be a matter of hanging on after others have let go."[11]

I believe that we all love a winner because deep in our DNA, in the heart of our being, is the spirit of a creature who knows how to succeed. That is why, when we see success, we identify with it. Remember that you are here on earth because you are already a winner. You began life with what it takes to fulfill your purpose. You can be hopeful because success is predictable, and your future is inevitable. If you persevere in following the laws of creation, you will succeed because your success is good for God.

Perseverance is also necessary because, as I mentioned previously, we often have to develop our gift for a long time before we are paid for it. Don't let that deter you—just keep working on your gift. Some people want to be great right away, but they need to start small. Practice your gift at every opportunity. Work your gift. Persevere.

Thought: Perseverance is the power to endure, to hold on, in spite of everything.

Reading: Isaiah 40:28–31

---

10. "Bahamas Wins Men's 4x400 Relay," Associated Press, August 10, 2012, reported by ESPN, https://www.espn.com/olympics/summer/2012/trackandfield/story/_/id/8257060/2012-london-olympics-bahamas-halts-us-streak-men-4x400-relay.
11. William Feather, "William Feather: Quotes," Goodreads, https://www.goodreads.com/quotes/346897-success-seems-to-be-largely-a-matter-of-hanging-on.

—Day 65—

TEN KEYS FOR PERSONAL SUCCESS: #10 PRAYER

"Your will be done on earth as it is in heaven."
—Luke 11:2 (NKJV)

In today's devotion, we look at the tenth key for personal success, *prayer,* which refers to our need for spiritual reserves.

To be successful, we must have a daily relationship with our Creator. That's what prayer is. To pray is to constantly stay connected to, and to petition, the Source of our purpose and gifting. We need to go to the One who gave us our gift to receive strength and guidance to deploy it. In a coming devotion, we'll talk about what it means to connect with our Source in the development of our personal character.

In Luke 11:2–4, Jesus gave us a model for prayer. You don't have to repeat the words of this prayer exactly, but you should use them as a pattern. Prayer is approaching God in order to ask Him to accomplish His will on the earth. And Jesus taught us how to fulfill this purpose.

Earlier, we talked about the need to be alone and to quiet our life in order to discover our gift. In the book of Isaiah, the Creator says, *"I make known the end from the beginning"* (Isaiah 46:10). In other words, "I show you who you have been from the beginning." So, again, if you are seeking your purpose or other guidance, why not spend a little time away from other people? You might go on a walk and ask the Creator to come with you. He wants to reveal or reinforce your true purpose and gift. Say, "God, let's go on a gift-finding walk." Then, regularly stay connected to Him as He reveals that purpose to you.

Additionally, regularly read the rest of the Manufacturer's Manual, which will help to guide you in your prayers. And read it not only as a devotional book but also in order to learn and remind yourself of the laws and principles of creation. Ask God to show you His laws, and then act on what you learn. We can follow the example of King David, who prayed:

> *Teach me,* LORD, *the way of your decrees,*
> *that I may follow it to the end.*
> *Give me understanding, so that I may keep your law*
> *and obey it with all my heart.*
> *Direct me in the path of your commands,*
> *for there I find delight.*
> *Turn my heart toward your statutes*
> *and not toward selfish gain.*
> *Turn my eyes away from worthless things;*
> *preserve my life according to your word.*
> *Fulfill your promise to your servant,*
> *so that you may be feared.*
> *Take away the disgrace I dread,*
> *for your laws are good.*
> *How I long for your precepts!*
> *In your righteousness preserve my life.*
> (Psalm 119:33–40)

Thought: To be successful, we must have a daily relationship with our Creator.

Reading: Luke 11:2–4 (NKJV)

—Day 66—
PROTECTING YOUR SUCCESS

> *"Physical training is of some value, but godliness has value for all things, holding promise for both the present life and the life to come."* —1 Timothy 4:8

As you pursue your purpose and experience success, don't expect your success to carry you in life.

That might seem like a surprising statement, so let me explain what I mean: Many people can't handle achievement well because the accompanying responsibility, rewards, and stakes weigh too heavily on them. People can fall into all kinds of moral and ethical problems when they are successful because they suddenly feel all-powerful and unrestrained. They don't realize that they are setting themselves up for a disastrous fall. Your gift is never a threat to your success—but a lack of character is. Throughout history, many leaders who failed did not fail because they were short on gifts but because they were short on character. Theodore Roosevelt said, "Character, in the long run, is the decisive factor in the life of an individual and of nations alike."[12]

A person who has talent but lacks character can be unstable and unreliable. Some people have ability, but they don't have "availability." They're gifted, but they can't be counted on to contribute their gift consistently. Nothing is more frustrating to people who are involved in a joint endeavor than dealing with a member of the group who is extremely talented but undependable. They cannot predict if the person will be present—physically or otherwise—to

---

12. Theodore Roosevelt, Theodore Roosevelt Rotunda, American Museum of Natural History, https://www.amnh.org/exhibitions/permanent/theodore-roosevelt-memorial/roosevelt-rotunda.

carry out their responsibilities. If the person doesn't show up, the endeavor can be jeopardized.

Talent without character is like a shooting star. It shines brightly for a moment but then is gone. Sometimes, people come on the public scene who have a brilliant intellect, a sparkling personality, or dazzling good looks. They seem to have all the right ingredients for success. But then, sometime later—it may be two weeks, a year, or several years—they seem to drop out of sight, and we wonder where they went. We find out that they quickly burned out due to a character issue that destroyed their reputation and potential.

In contrast, character is like the sun—it shines consistently and reliably. On days when we experience cloudy skies or pouring rain, the sun is still shining from its consistent position in the solar system. People with character have these qualities of consistency and reliability. Consequently, they have a positive effect on the lives of those around them.

Attaining true success is thus not just about exercising the gift the Creator has implanted within us and attracting financial prosperity but also about having the character of the Creator who made us. His character and His laws go together. The only way to protect what you hope to accomplish in your life, and what you have already accomplished, is to develop and maintain strong personal character. Character development produces within us an internal environment for success.

Thought: Attaining true success is not just about exercising the gift the Creator has implanted within us but also about having the character of the Creator.

Reading: 2 Peter 1:5–7

—Day 67—
IN SYNC WITH THE CREATOR

> *"All things have been created through* [Jesus Christ] *and for him. He is before all things, and in him all things hold together."* —Colossians 1:16–17

Jesus said, *"What good will it be for someone to gain the whole world, yet forfeit their soul? Or what can anyone give in exchange for their soul?"* (Matthew 16:26). In effect, a person can "gain the world" through the power and riches associated with success but, at the same time, forfeit their soul—the very core of their being—by ignoring or betraying their own character. In doing so, they can lose their impact and their longevity—not to mention the reason for their very existence. That is a tragic waste of life.

For example, if we violate the laws of the Creator in our relationships with other people, we can shut down our seed of success. Success is holistic. All the laws and principles work together. Concerning relationships, Jesus said, *"If you are offering your gift* [to God] *at the altar and there remember that your brother or sister has something against you, leave your gift there in front of the altar. First go and be reconciled to them; then come and offer your gift"* (Matthew 5:23–24). Therefore, if our relationships with other people are not right, we can't walk around saying, "I'm exercising the principle of giving, but I'm not receiving." That's not the issue. The issue is, do we see the whole picture, and are we applying it?

It is like planting a seed in the ground and then pouring kerosene on it once it begins to grow. We may have used sound principles of development such as providing the seed with soil, water, and light, but now we are doing something that negates the effect of those principles. When we aren't experiencing success or our success begins to wane, the reason could be as simple as the negation of a principle.

Our whole life has to be in sync with the Creator's laws and principles. That's why I can't afford to hold anything against anyone. If people insult me, I need to protect my heart and forgive them. This is the reason Jesus told us to love our enemies. (See Matthew 5:43–45.) We love our enemies because we don't want hatred or a desire for revenge to shut down our relationships, impacting our purpose and our journey of success. I will never get in a fight with anyone because I have to guard my relationship with the Creator and allow my own tree to grow. How others respond to me is their own responsibility. I need to focus on what I'm supposed to do. Sometimes we think that when we forgive someone, they're supposed to forgive us also. That's not what the Manufacturer's Manual says. It just says we are to forgive them. (See, for example, Matthew 6:12; 18:21–35.) To forgive means to release the other person. That means the issue is now on them. You are clear in your relationship with them and with the Creator.

Thought: Our whole life has to be in sync with the Creator's laws and principles.

Reading: John 17:20–23

—Day 68—

HOW HUMAN BEINGS LOST CHARACTER

"I have the desire to do what is good, but I cannot carry it out." —Romans 7:18

Why is having consistently good character often a struggle for people? Why do we find ourselves doing or saying things that aren't right? Understanding the answer to these questions and learning to establish character in our life starts with going back to how we were made in creation.

First, the order that the Creator set for us is *character before power.* When we return to character, we return to the natural state in which we were meant to function. We have seen that we were made in the image and likeness of God, and that one of God's first instructions to human beings was, *"Be fruitful and increase in number; fill the earth and subdue it"* (Genesis 1:28). The whole world was to be filled with men, women, and children who manifested the nature of God as they exercised their unique purpose and gift. Accordingly, we should develop an environment conducive to demonstrating that nature. Internally, we should develop the mindset and qualities of character. Externally, we should create a community atmosphere that promotes and upholds ethical standards, such as integrity and justice.

We talked earlier about how the first human beings rejected God's law. Ironically, human beings lost their ability to consistently manifest the Creator's nature because the first man and woman heeded the false accusation that God wasn't treating them with true character—that He was not being just. When His trustworthiness was called into question, they made a decision to doubt His authenticity. Then, for the sake of gaining power for themselves, they broke a key law He had established for them. (See Genesis 3.)

The principle that the first human beings violated had been designed to protect them so that they would not suffer the consequences of living outside of God's nature. In breaking this principle, they went against the very means that would have safeguarded them. Because they *chose* to live outside of God's nature, their character became warped. This indicates that, in some way, their character did not depend on nature alone—it also required an ongoing decision to remain in that nature. Today, we face the same type of decision: Will we live by our established principles, beliefs, values, moral standards, and ethical code? This is a choice we make on a daily basis.

The first humans' tragic decision caused humanity to suffer the consequences of a loss of God's true nature—including the onset of strife, sickness, and physical death. The fundamental source of all of humanity's deficiencies and problems was—and is—its rejection of the Creator's principles. This rejection is what the Scriptures call "sin." It is why human nature is described as being "fallen." Human nature once existed on a high ethical plane, but it descended into a place where it often manifests only a fraction of its former state.

In the next two devotions, we'll examine some results of the loss of character and then explore God's life-changing plan for restoring human beings to character.

Thought: The order that the Creator set for us is *character before power.*

Reading: Romans 7:14–24

—Day 69—

RESULTS OF THE LOSS OF CHARACTER

"We all, like sheep, have gone astray, each of us has turned to our own way." —Isaiah 53:6

When the first human beings rejected the character and law of God, there were several devastating results. First, because humanity lost God's true nature, it now has only a distorted image of that nature. The principal traits of fallen human beings are the opposite of genuine character: inconsistency, unpredictability, unfaithfulness, compromise, unjustness, prejudice, untrustworthiness, domination, vindictiveness, unforgiveness, cruelty, and so forth. All societies of the world suffer the symptoms of humanity's loss of character.

All human corruption stems from our loss of God's character as an intrinsic element of our own nature. Human beings are still capable of exercising moral conduct, but this involves making the continual decision to embrace strong convictions and values. And we are all inconsistent in this endeavor, because sound character is no longer natural to us.

Another result of human beings' rejection of God's image is that they lost their own essence. They became confused about their self-image and self-worth—who they were, what they were born to be, and how they were to live. They no longer had a clear sense of purpose and meaning in the world. And they forfeited the feeling of acceptance and worth that comes from being in unbroken relationship with their Creator.

Without character, human beings also became unstable. This is why it is often hard for us to depend on others. Many people neglect to keep their promises. For example, on their wedding day, a couple gets dressed up, stands in front of a clergyperson or a justice of the peace, and makes promises to each other such as, "I will love and cherish you until I die!" Then, at some point after the honeymoon, the husband or wife may lose interest and leave—sometimes to run off with someone else. Such heartbreak occurs because many people are unstable and inconsistent. They haven't made the conscious decision to establish strong values and truly commit to them.

If someone is unstable, it doesn't matter what they promise—you can't trust it. As the biblical writer James said, "*Can both fresh water and salt water flow from the same spring? My brothers and sisters, can a fig tree bear olives, or a grapevine bear figs? Neither can a salt spring produce fresh water*" (James 3:11–12). If the source hasn't changed, the result will be the same. James also wrote, "*The one who doubts is like a wave of the sea, blown and tossed by the wind.... Such a person is double-minded and unstable in all they do*" (James 1:6–8). An unstable person is like the waves of the sea—unpredictable, changeable.

That is why, when we meet people who have strong character, we admire and love them. It is because they are a picture of our original self. A person of character gives us a glimpse of what all human beings used to be like and what most of us, deep down, desire to be like. Let us become inspired to return to our true self—the image of God.

Thought: All human corruption stems from our loss of God's character as an intrinsic element of our own nature.

Reading: Isaiah 53:5–6

—Day 70—
THE RESTORATION OF CHARACTER

"Therefore, if anyone is in Christ, he is a new creation; old things have passed away; behold, all things have become new." —2 Corinthians 5:17 (NKJV)

I previously described how the Creator's plans for human beings did not include allowing them to languish in a state in which they lacked His nature—and experienced all the resulting consequences. In His faithfulness and trustworthiness, He initiated a plan to restore humanity to Himself. This plan involved giving us a renewed nature, one by which we would again be able to share His character and consistently follow His life-giving principles.

He accomplished this plan through Jesus of Nazareth, also called Jesus Christ. God testified about Him, *"This is my Son, whom I love; with him I am well pleased"* (Matthew 3:17). Jesus said, *"I and the Father are one"* (John 10:30). Jesus was God's Son because He came from God, He was one with God, and He fully manifested God's character on earth. One of Jesus's disciples wrote about Him:

> *In the beginning was the Word, and the Word was with God, and the Word was God. He was with God in the beginning. Through him all things were made; without him nothing was made that has been made. In him was life, and that life was the light of all mankind.... The Word became flesh and made his dwelling among us.* (John 1:1–4, 14)

And Paul of Tarsus wrote, *"For in Christ all the fullness of the Deity lives in bodily form"* (Colossians 2:9). Jesus had the same nature and Spirit as God. And His purpose for coming to the earth was to restore the image of God in us. The Scriptures are very clear that we need a new nature: *"No one can enter the kingdom of God unless they are born of water and the Spirit"* (John 3:5).

Therefore, Jesus came to give us back our character. No one can be restored to the Creator's nature except through Him. (See John 14:6.) Jesus Christ, as the Son of God, was the only One who could represent both the Creator and His created beings in order to fix the breach between the two and bring about full reconciliation and restoration.

When Jesus died on the cross, He paid the price for our fallen human nature. He also paid the price for all the times when we ourselves have acted contrary to the character and laws of our Creator. When we acknowledge and accept what He did for us, we are restored to God and receive His nature within us once again. This enables us to experience a lasting transformation by which we can manifest His image and develop genuine character according to His principles. In this life, we can expect to experience a process of ongoing growth and maturation in the way we manifest the Creator's nature. God described His plan of restoration in this way: *"I will put my law in their minds and write it on their hearts. I will be their God, and they will be my people"* (Jeremiah 31:33).

Thought: When we acknowledge and accept what Christ did for us, we are restored to God and receive His nature within us once again.

Reading: 2 Corinthians 5:14–21

—Day 71—

AGREEING WITH GOD

> *"If we confess our sins, he is faithful and just and will forgive us our sins and purify us from all unrighteousness."*
>
> —1 John 1:9

We have seen that whenever we go against the Creator's law, it doesn't hurt God—His peace and integrity remain intact. However, it hurts us and shuts us down. After we are restored to God and receive His nature, what should we do if we once again violate one of His laws on the path to maturity? How do we get back on track so we can move forward and walk with character?

I grew up believing that when you confessed your sin, it meant that you were supposed to say what you had done and tell God how sorry you were about it. However, when I was in college, I took a course in Hebrew. In one class, my professor, Dr. Hayden, was discussing the translation of various words, one of which was *confession*. I learned that the Hebrew word for confession doesn't really mean to bring up anything with God. Dr. Hayden explained it in this way: "The word confess means that you agree with God. If your heart condemns you, if the Lord says in your heart that what you did was wrong, you just agree it's wrong."

We often try to explain to God why we did something wrong and offer an excuse or justification for it, but this means we have not confessed in the sense of agreeing that it is wrong. We shouldn't try to explain it but simply say, "God, You are right. This is wrong. I have gone against Your law."

Another word we hear in relation to sin is *repent*. The acts of confession and repentance are distinct. To confess means to agree that something is wrong, while to repent means to go in the other direction. Thus, to repent means to change your mind about what you did, and to intend not to do it again. When we do this, we reopen access to the benefits of obedience to God's laws.

You may think, for example, that you're getting away with some private things God doesn't know about, but God knows everything. He sees what we're doing when no one else is watching. If you're secretly flirting with violating God's laws, He is giving you an opportunity to sort this thing out now because, eventually, it's going to harm you and the fulfillment of your purpose.

I want you to think carefully about this. Going against God's law can shut down the entire success principle. Whenever your conscience tells you that what you're doing is not right, just say, "God, You're right," and then immediately cease doing it. You can turn away from it. Whenever you do this, you reinforce character in your life.

In the next few devotions, we will talk about how to intentionally establish values and standards for our life to build character.

Thought: When we confess and repent of our wrongdoing, we reopen access to the benefits of obedience to God's laws.

Reading: 1 John 1:5–10

— Day 72 —

A PERSONAL SECURITY SYSTEM

"Above all else, guard your heart, for everything you do flows from it." —Proverbs 4:23

In an earlier devotion, I said that we shouldn't expect our success to carry us because, if we are not careful, we can misuse the power and influence that come with it, leading to ethical or moral failure. Therefore, instead of expecting our success to carry us, we need to let our success be carried by our character. Developing character will also enable us to cultivate enduring positive influence as we fulfill our purpose—a topic we will discuss more fully in the final section of this devotional.

Having good character is like having a personal security system for your life. Many people install security devices in their homes and places of business to protect them from thieves who would try to steal from them and from intruders who would try to harm their family members or employees. We can "install" character in our lives so that it will work like a security system. We do this by focusing on the Manufacturer's laws and principles and then developing values and standards that correspond to them. These values and standards will alert us to, and protect us from, the negative effects of various outside influences—such as life's pressures, difficulties, and temptations. Negative outside influences can threaten our success by invading our life and stealing our willpower, common sense, and better judgment. Values and standards also safeguard us from internal "intruders"—our own human frailties that cause us to rationalize immoral behavior and take ethical shortcuts. A person of principle does not change their values and standards, no matter the circumstances.

To better understand the nature of values, let's look at two related definitions:

Values are ideas, principles, and qualities on which you personally place high worth. A value is a belief—in something or someone—that you esteem, on its own merits. For instance, you may value the idea of giving charitable aid to families whose wage earner has been laid off from work, or you may value the principle of "equal justice under law" or the quality of courage.

Values are standards or ideals that determine your conduct or policy. To use a simple example, suppose you own a diamond ring, and you know the market value of diamonds and want to protect your asset. The value you place on your diamond ring will both predict and affect your behavior toward it. If you truly value it as a possession, you will keep it clean and put it in a safe place when you're not wearing it. You may even check on it periodically to make sure it has not been lost or stolen.

Successful people adhere to a value system by which they consider options for conduct, make decisions, and take action. They are identified by the positive values that they consider worthy and by which they have determined to live. For positive values to make a difference in your life and your journey of success, you must embrace certain steps. In our next devotion, we will talk about what those steps are.

Thought: Instead of expecting our success to carry us, we need to let our success be carried by our character.

Reading: Proverbs 4:20–27

—DAY 73—

DEVELOPING VALUES

"As [a person] *thinks in his heart, so is he."*

—Proverbs 23:7 (NKJV)

In today's devotion, we turn our attention to the process of developing values for our life.

The first step is to *identify your values*. Carefully think through what you truly value and then express your values in writing. Your values determine how you intend to conduct yourself. They are your guides for living, doing business, relating to other people, and relating to life. You need to settle them in your heart and mind so that you will have standards to live by. You must clarify what you will and will not do.

Keep in mind that identifying and articulating your values is usually not accomplished in one sitting. It takes a thoughtful evaluation of your purpose, convictions, and vision for the future. And, as you increasingly come to understand your inherent purpose and gifts, you should refine the written statement of your values.

Second, *believe in your values*. Values are not ideals to which you give mere mental assent, because they are an indispensable part of your ability to live a life of purpose and character. Therefore, you should embrace values you can truly believe in and have confidence in—those you affirm and by which you desire to live.

Third, you must believe in your values to the point that you *"receive" your values*. In other words, you internalize them so that they can become a vital part of who you are. You receive your values by reviewing them often, thinking about them, and affirming their place in your life.

The fourth step is to *adhere to your values*. These values become your parameters, or framework, for living. You should measure everything against those parameters. There is an important distinction between compromising one's beliefs and making a concession on an opinion so that a group can come to a consensus. In those circumstances, we are not to be uncompromising for its own sake. However, when moral issues are clearly at stake, we must steadfastly hold on to our values and ethical code.

Thus, you must not only believe in and internalize your values but also put them into practice if they are to guide your life. Periodically take time to evaluate if you are living according to your stated values.

Finally, you need to be able to *share your values* with others in any corporate entity of which you are a part—whether it is a family, a business, an organization, a nation, or another group. Remember that a personal vision can be fulfilled only in conjunction with other people's visions as you share a common purpose. Similarly, corporate values are effective only when they become the personal values of all the members. Every member of an organization needs to be in general agreement with the corporate values.

If you are a leader who sets a corporate vision, you should remind people often of what is valuable to the community and what is valuable to you personally. Values must not only be heard but also "seen"—in other words, demonstrated, especially by you.

Thought: Are you living according to your stated values?

Reading: James 1:22–25

—Day 74—

INTEGRATING YOUR THOUGHTS, WORDS, AND ACTIONS

"Let us not love with words or speech but with actions and in truth." —1 John 3:18

Today, many people lack a framework for evaluating the suitability and consequences of their conduct and policies. Our framework of values becomes our measure not only of *whether* we will do something but also, if so, *how* we will conduct ourselves while doing it.

To build a framework for personal character, we must develop standards for our life that are derived from our values. After you have developed a written statement of your values, you should also write down your personal standards or principles for living. Writing down the ideas and behaviors on which you place high worth will help you to identify and clarify them. In addition, if your standards are recorded in written form, you can put them in an accessible place (such as a computer file or a folder in your desk) so that you can continually refer to them.

Here are some examples of written standards that reflect values. A married person who values the institution of marriage might translate that value into a moral standard in this way: "I value the institution of marriage, so my corresponding personal moral standard, or principle for living, is that I will be faithful, and remain faithful, to my spouse." A businessperson who values honesty might translate that value into the following standard: "I esteem the quality of honesty; therefore, my corresponding moral conviction, or principle, is that I will always tell the truth to my customers and never overcharge them or bill them for services that were not performed," or "I will treat my employees justly by giving them fair wages and ensuring the safety of their work environment."

The words *integrate* and *integrity* are both derived from the Latin word *integer,* meaning "whole" and "entire." Thus, one definition of *integrate* is "to form, coordinate, or blend into a functioning or unified whole."[13] Having character means making a *continual* effort to integrate your thoughts, words, and actions. You should be able to declare, "What I say, what I do, and who I am are the same."

A person of principle possesses beliefs so strong that they are willing to sacrifice for them—to experience the loss of popularity, friendships, colleagues, financial gain, and success for their sake. I believe such a quality must be reintroduced in our society by individuals of genuine principle.

In conjunction with making sacrifices, we must impose daily discipline upon ourselves so that we will remain aligned with our convictions and continue to adhere to our principles. Discipline begins with our mind. Again, it involves setting priorities for ourselves that determine our choices and direct our behavior. The key to being disciplined is to set parameters for your life in relation to both your moral standards and your daily activities—what you will and will not accept for yourself, and what you will and will not participate in. We are self-disciplined when we understand that there are purposes and goals in life that are immeasurably greater than temporary pleasures, secondary objectives, and everyday distractions.

Thought: What are your personal standards or principles for living, based on your values?

Reading: 1 John 3:16–24

13. Merriam-Webster.com Dictionary, s.v. "integrate," https://www.merriam-webster.com/dictionary/integrate.

—Day 75—

VISION AND VALUES

"For where your treasure is, there your heart will be also."
—Matthew 6:21

An important principle to remember is that there's no "break" in life from character. There is no point at which we will have "arrived" so that we no longer have to concern ourselves with values and principles. We must therefore keep vigil over our character. For instance, it is very easy to be tempted to lie. Suppose you were laid off from your job, and you found some short-term work through a temporary agency. Then, at a social function, you meet a wealthy business executive who asks you, "So, what do you do for a living?" You don't want to seem inferior, so you inflate your job description. Character requires daily maintenance because every day—and often many times throughout the day—our character will be tested.

If you endeavor to do what is right, I guarantee that you will eventually emerge at the top. Don't worry about people who take shortcuts or compromise to get ahead. Don't be jealous of them. They will ultimately fail.

In this regard, for the next few devotions, I want to further explore the relationship between vision and values. I often say, "Leaders stand *for* something—vision. Leaders stand *on* something—values." This statement is true for anyone pursuing their purpose because everyone is a leader in their own gifting and domain. And, of these two elements, values are of higher importance than vision. If we don't have an active commitment to our values, moral standards, principles, discipline, and ethical code, all of our endeavors will be weakened—and may even be nullified.

Your vision should be an interpretation of your values in the sense that it should reflect and communicate them. Earlier in this devotional, we talked about how someone might discover their gift by recognizing that they are angry about the fact that young people are living on the streets without any sense of purpose. That person's vision might be to help young people who are members of gangs that are undermining their community to become engaged in positive activities that will build up the community instead. The vision communicates that this individual values the lives of young people and also values improving the quality of life in their community.

Similarly, an organization's vision reflects its corporate values. For instance, suppose the vision of a home-based business was to create exquisitely embroidered garments to sell to specialty stores, the proceeds of which would supplement the family's income. This vision communicates that the business, through its owner, values creativity, quality, enterprise, and financial stability.

Therefore, when leaders in politics, religion, education, business, economics, sports, and other fields invest their time and money in a vision, that vision can be used as a measure for assessing their principal values. As Jesus of Nazareth said, *"For where your treasure is, there your heart will be also."*

Thought: Your vision should be an interpretation of your values in the sense that it should reflect and communicate them.

Reading: Matthew 6:19–24

—Day 76—

VALUES ATTRACT SIMILAR VALUES

"Do two walk together unless they have agreed to do so?"
—Amos 3:3

Your vision is only as safe as the values that undergird it. If you cherish a great vision but don't value the principles that would enable you to realize it, you may as well not pursue that vision. There needs to be a marriage of purpose and principles. You have to *know* your purpose, but you must *live by* your principles. In this sense, vision may be compared to the head, and values to the heart. You should take the advice of the ancient proverb that says, *"Above all else, guard your heart, for everything you do flows from it"* (Proverbs 4:23).

It is generally the case that people who hold particular values are drawn to other people who hold the same or similar values. Applying this point to personal relationships, we know that friendships are forged among people who have similar interests and preferences.

My close friends and associates share my values. As I expressed previously, there are other people with whom I am unable to associate. My experiences with them have revealed that they don't value the things that I value; in fact, sometimes they value things that I believe are detrimental. That doesn't mean that I intentionally snub them. Yet, as a leader, I have to protect my character, and a close tie with them would not only be ethically unhealthy for me, but it might also give the impression to others that I support their values.

Values are so important that they should be the basis of our key associations. The same point applies to corporate relationships—for example, companies doing business with one another and governments making agreements and treaties with other countries and supporting various international causes.

When considering an association, we should ask ourselves, "What overt or underlying values are involved in this decision? What binding alliances am I making?"

While there is no such thing as an "ethical community," there is such a thing as a community of ethical people. Corporately, the people agree on the values by which they are going to live. That agreement is what creates a culture of morality. And that moral culture becomes the source of ethics for the community. An ethical culture always begins with individuals' personal commitment to live according to strong values.

This is why individual leaders and organizations alike should protect themselves against ethical breaches by setting strong values for themselves. An organization's governing board should decide what types of policies it will and will not sanction. A business should determine what standards it will not compromise on. A family should decide what media content it will and will not allow into the home. A corporate entity that has not established values for itself lacks moral protection. It is like a city without walls from ancient times that has left itself vulnerable to deadly attack by enemy armies.

Thought: Values are so important that they should be the basis of our key associations.

Reading: 1 Peter 3:8

—Day 77—

THE PROCESS OF VISION

"Make every effort to keep the unity of the Spirit through the bond of peace." —Ephesians 4:3

It has been said that "the process is as important as the product," and this is certainly true in regard to fulfilling one's vision. Years ago, my organization decided to construct a large building called the Diplomat Center. I envisioned how it would be used to teach people about their purpose as leaders. So, I was excited about it, and I was caught up with securing the property, raising the money, and working long hours to see it come to fruition. However, one day, I sensed that God was saying to me, "I am not pleased with you." I was confused, so I asked, "What are You talking about? I'm doing Your will. You told me to build the building." He said, "You're not leading the people. You are driving them." It broke my heart to realize that I had been driving the people who were involved in the vision, rather than inspiring them.

Then, I felt God saying, "You have passion, and passion is good, but you have no *com*passion. Stop everything. I want you to get your balance back." Deeply convicted, I went into a brief season of solitude in order to regain the balance between my passion and my compassion. The people in my organization were supposed to love this project, not just endure it. So, after reflecting on the situation, I had to go to the people and publicly ask them to forgive me for breaking the law of compassion. I explained to them that, from that point on, we would work together. My confession changed the whole spirit of the organization. People donated more money toward the project, and they also dedicated their time and their skills to see it accomplished.

The ethical issue I had to deal with was that I had been standing *for* something—the idea of how the new building would support the organization's vision—but I hadn't been standing *on* the values that were needed for the process of carrying it out. Again, having character requires more than discovering what you were born to do and pursuing the fulfillment of your vision; it involves pursuing the fulfillment of your vision in a way that corresponds with ethical principles.

One of my close friends is a distinguished gentleman named Dr. Richard Demeritte Jr. He and I met years ago when he was the ambassador to England from the Bahamas. He has also served as the ambassador to the European Union. Once, when we were talking together, he told me a time-honored value that his father had conveyed to him: "When in doubt, do what's right." This statement provides extremely valuable yet easy-to-remember ethical advice. When you are faced with a moral choice, just do what's right! A person of character should always live in that way.

Thought: When in doubt, do what's right!

Reading: Ephesians 4:1–6

—Day 78—

VISION GIVES MEANING TO PEOPLE—AND VALUES PRESERVE THAT VISION

"Where there is no vision, the people perish."
—Proverbs 29:18 (KJV)

Many leaders think that their goal should be to get people to believe in them. On the contrary, the goal of leaders should be to get people to believe in *themselves*—to provide an avenue through which they can discover meaning for their life and manifest their purpose through their personal vision. Helping people to do this requires balance on the part of the leader, because, when people are inspired by a leader's passion, they often confuse the vision with the leader. In this way, they think they are being drawn to the person. A leader of principle takes the focus off themself and puts it on the vision. It is the vision—not the leader—that gives people meaning. And it is the vision that will sustain the people's conviction, because that is where they will find their significance in serving their gift to others.

This shows how important it is for leaders to act on their convictions and not neglect their vision. Remember, when we pursue our own purpose, we actually help other people to find theirs. We should reflect on that responsibility because the opposite scenario can also occur. If we don't maintain our passion for our vision, the people may also lose their energy for their vision. When we feel like giving up and start talking about quitting, the people may also begin to lose their sense of purpose. When we lose our focus or our commitment to strong character, the people may lose their way in life. Therefore, we must keep vision and values prominent—other people are depending on us! Who are you currently helping to find meaning and purpose for their own life through your vision?

It is imperative that people stay focused on the vision rather than on the leader because of the danger that a cult of personality will develop. You must never allow people to become so attached to you that they begin to idolize you. How many organizations today have become defunct because they were run by leaders who were "worshipped" by their followers, so that everything fell apart when those leaders had a major moral failure? Leaders need to watch their pride in this respect, because pride can destroy them and their vision. Pride is what makes leaders think they *should* be idolized. They being to think the vision is all about them, that it's built around them, that its success is all up to them. Let us guard against such attitudes. Humility is a core quality of principled leaders. Cultivating an attitude of humility will help us protect ourselves and our vision.

Never forget that you and your vision have great significance. "Your" people—the people who are, or who will be, associated with your vision need you. Your character is vital to them. For their sake, as well as your own, commit to be a leader of principle.

Thought: The goal of leaders should be to provide an avenue through which people can discover meaning for their life and manifest their purpose through their personal vision.

Reading: Titus 1:7–8

—Day 79—
THE INFLUENCE OF SUCCESS

"Set an example for the believers in speech, in conduct, in love, in faith and in purity." —1 Timothy 4:12

One of the reasons we focus on success is because success naturally brings us influence with other people. Just as we were born to be a success in a domain of life, we were born to be an influence in that domain—and even beyond. On the journey of success, you will develop into a person who inspires and impacts others. You were meant to influence your family, community, business, government, and more in beneficial ways.

You will never have influence until you are successful, and you will never be successful until you have influence. The two are connected. Those who discover and understand who they are and what their life's purpose is will influence their environments more than their environments influence them. Once again, our goal should be to focus on fulfilling our purpose, which will lead to our becoming successful in the arena of our gifting. Then, when our success gives us influence, we are to use that influence for good in a variety of ways as our success increases.

Unfortunately, we have often confused influence with domination. There are many people, past and present, who have swayed others using threats and violence, but we don't call that true influence. We call it manipulation, oppression, or dictatorship. Nero, Hitler, and Idi Amin were all influential. They exerted their wills over people, but they were not leaders in the true sense. Leadership influence is a powerful instrument, and we must always be aware of its potential to bring either good or harm to others.

According to the Creator's original design, we're not supposed to dominate other people—we're supposed to have dominion *over the earth* and its resources. If we don't understand this distinction, we will manipulate and abuse others and frustrate the expression of their own God-given purpose and gift. The true nature of success is for other people to be attracted to our gift, which is deployed in their service. So, exerting proper influence means inspiring others through the gift that we have been given.

As we discussed previously, when you find your unique gift or special talent and commit to serving it to humanity, then your significance will cause people to seek you out. You will become an influence through exercising your gift rather than through manipulation. And the more you become a person whose gift is valued, the greater your influence will be.

I was invited to Las Vegas to speak to a group of twelve people who, combined, control over $100 billion. That day, I was their teacher from 8:00 a.m. until 4:00 p.m. This is the type of person I am influencing just from pursuing my purpose and exercising my gift. You, too, can have great influence if you follow the laws and principles that I have learned and have outlined in this devotional—again, not solely for your own sake but for the sake of serving your gift to the world. Remember, a tree that bears fruit does not eat its own harvest; that harvest is meant to be shared for the good of others.

Thought: Just as we were born to be a success in a domain of life, we were born to be an influence in that domain.

Reading: 1 Timothy 4

—Day 80—

WHAT IS INFLUENCE?

"Join together in following my example, brothers and sisters, and just as you have us as a model, keep your eyes on those who live as we do." —Philippians 3:17

For over thirty years, I have dedicated myself to the study of the subject of leadership. After thousands of hours of studying, researching, and reading hundreds of books on the subject, I determined to develop my own comprehensive definition of leadership as I have come to understand it. This definition incorporates the principal ingredients and components that I believe give birth to and sustain true leadership. It can be applied by anyone who desires to discover and release the gift within them, with its corresponding leadership potential:

> Leadership is the capacity to *influence* others through *inspiration* motivated by a *passion,* generated by a *vision,* produced by a *conviction,* ignited by a *purpose.*

The best way to approach this definition and appreciate its practical application is to start the process at the end of the statement. As you might have guessed, the process begins with an individual's discovery of a personal purpose that, when captured, ignites a conviction. This conviction generates a vision in the person's heart that stirs a passion. The force of this person's passionate pursuit of their vision inspires others who are stirred to participate in and cooperate with the vision. This ultimate effect is called "influence."

The purest form of leadership is influence through inspiration. I think of inspiration as the divine deposit of destiny in the heart of a person. If inspiration is the key to influence and thus the source of leadership, how do we inspire others? What is the source of inspiration? Simply put, the source of inspiration is *passion*. This component is the heart of influence and generates our energy and resilience.

As I mentioned earlier, passion is birthed from a revelation of where we are headed in life. When a person discovers a sense of purpose, it produces a passion for pursuing it, and that passion is what inspires other people to want to join in the pursuit. Then, as people are inspired, their thinking and their lives are naturally influenced. Inspiration is an invitation to pursue something that is higher and better than we have had before—changing the status quo, creating something new, finding a solution to a problem, and so forth—and, in the process, to gain a sense of meaning and significance for our life.

Those who exercise positive influence don't try to prove themselves to others. They are more concerned with "manifesting" themselves, or revealing the purpose they were born to fulfill. To sum up, the essence of leadership influence is the ability to motivate other people to take action and effect change, and you can't influence if you don't inspire. You can't inspire if you don't have passion, and you won't have passion unless you are convinced about your purpose, convictions, and vision.

Thought: Leadership is the capacity to *influence* others through *inspiration* motivated by a *passion*, generated by a *vision*, produced by a *conviction*, ignited by a *purpose*.

Reading: Philippians 3:7–21

—Day 81—
JESUS'S INFLUENCE

"I have set you an example that you should do as I have done for you."
—John 13:15

Jesus of Nazareth became successful before He was influential. He grew up in a little village. Archeologists have excavated the area where the original town of Nazareth stood. Based on the results of this excavation work, Nazareth has been described as "an out-of-the-way hamlet of around 50 houses on a patch of about four acres.... It was evidently populated by Jews of modest means."[14] Nazareth was really a small settlement—humble and without much influence in the surrounding world.

When Nathanael, who became one of Jesus's disciples, initially heard that Jesus was from that small town, he said, *"Nazareth! Can anything good come from there?"* (John 1:46). Later, when Jesus was living in the town of Capernaum, people said, *"Is this not Jesus, the son of Joseph, whose father and mother we know? How can he now say, 'I came down from heaven'?"* (John 6:42). In essence, they were saying, "Who do You think You are?" They were focused only on the hometown and family from which Jesus came; they didn't understand His purpose, which transcended those elements.

When Jesus was about to begin His ministry, He knew that if He were to fulfill His purpose, He had to succeed at something, which would give Him influence. So what did He do? He went looking for a problem, and He found one. As I wrote earlier, success often begins with our identifying a problem to solve. What was the problem Jesus found? It was three young fishermen sitting

14. Diaa Hadid, "First Jesus-Era House Found in Nazareth," NBC News, December 21, 2009, https://www.nbcnews.com/id/wbna34511072.

on the beach with an empty boat. These men were professionals, but they hadn't caught any fish, and they didn't know what to do about it. So Jesus addressed their problem using one of His gifts: the gift of exercising dominion over the earth. He told the fishermen to go back out onto the water and try again. This time, they caught so many fish that their boats were in danger of sinking. He had solved their problem. What happened after that? *"They pulled their boats up on shore, left everything and followed him"* (Luke 5:11; see also verses 1–10). That's influence.

Jesus became successful by exercising His gifts in various ways, making Him influential. Jesus became a celebrity—He was celebrated. Suddenly, people were listening to Him. Large crowds began to seek Him out. Many people even got to the point where they said, "We will follow You." Your influence is manifested when other people change their priorities for your priorities. In this sense, influence can be defined as the capacity to cause other people to listen to you or to follow you.

Thought: Your influence is manifested when other people change their priorities for your priorities.

Reading: John 13:1–15

—DAY 82—

THE INFLUENCE OF WEALTH AND WISDOM

"King Solomon was greater in riches and wisdom than all the other kings of the earth. The whole world sought audience with Solomon to hear the wisdom God had put in his heart."
—1 Kings 10:23–24

Success, in itself, is a major key to having influence. A second key, which is related to the first, is wealth, or prosperity. Wealthy people have influence. If we fail, people are much less likely to listen to us (though trial and error and setbacks can be part of the process of success). If we're broke, people don't usually look to us as an example or seek to talk with us.

There is nothing wrong with gaining wealth, even though many people have been taught to think that there is. The problem is not wealth but rather how some people go about gaining it and the attitude that they have toward it. That's why I prefer to define wealth by giving it a criterion: honest wealth. Honest wealth makes you influential.

Recall Moses's statement to the people whom he led: *"Remember the LORD your God, for it is he who gives you the ability to produce wealth"* (Deuteronomy 8:18). Biblical exhortations concerning money, including Paul's statement that *"the love of money is a root of all kinds of evil"* (1 Timothy 6:10), do not warn against possessing money or wealth but rather against allowing money or wealth to possess us. Loving money at the expense of the dignity, value, and welfare of others is an abuse of our ability to obtain wealth. Power, authority, position, money, and so forth are meant to be tools that enable us to achieve a noble purpose—not to serve selfish or dishonorable ends.

God told Abraham, the father of the Israelites, in effect, "I'm going to bless you and make you a blessing." Abraham became the richest man in his region. Why would God want to make him rich? In order to give him influence. Abraham was very comfortable with the power that he had. He was not proud in relation to it, but he was grateful for it and handled it responsibly. He had influence with others, and he credited that influence to God. (See, for example, Genesis 12:1–3; 13.)

We can see that there are different ways to become influential. David's son King Solomon inherited wealth and increased in riches. He also had a gift that drew people to him: extraordinary wisdom. Solomon became the most influential king in the history of Israel, and other rulers of the earth traveled from afar to have an audience with him. (See 1 Kings 10:1–13, 23–24.) I believe that wisdom and wealth always go together. I think that's why Solomon did not ask God for wealth. He asked God for wisdom, which will always attract wealth. (See 1 Kings 3:5–15.)

Let us therefore always consider the aspect of influence whenever we think of success and its effects. Again, we need to focus on pursuing our gift in our domain while following God's principles and asking Him to give us wisdom for gaining wealth. As we do this, we will naturally gain and exert influence. And, if we become successful and influential in one area, we often become influential in other areas as well.

Thought: Power, authority, position, money, and so forth are meant to be tools that enable us to achieve a noble purpose.

Reading: 1 Kings 3:5–15

—Day 83—

THE IMPACT OF INFLUENCE, PART 1

"We seemed like grasshoppers in our own eyes, and we looked the same to them." —Numbers 13:33

The influence we exert can impact the lives of other people in significant ways. Over the next several devotions, we will explore some of those ways so that we can be aware of them and act responsibly in regard to our influence over others.

One way we can impact others through influence is by transforming people's outlook to the point where their perspective becomes completely different from the way they formerly thought. For example, someone might use rhetorical skills to convince people that what they believed was good is actually evil, and vice versa—altering their values and conduct. Such influence is a tremendous power that we need to acknowledge and discipline in our own life, ensuring that we do not abuse it—especially since a change in mindset almost always leads to a change in behavior.

Nevertheless, an enlightened perspective is a gift that we can give to other people. When Harriet Beecher Stowe wrote the novel *Uncle Tom's Cabin,* she changed the mindset of tens of thousands of people who had been either neutral toward the institution of slavery in America or accepting of it. By putting a personal face on the issue, she showed that slaves were people rather than "property," so that many citizens began to support efforts to abolish slavery.

Another way that someone in a position of influence can impact the lives of others is by transferring their attitude to those who follow them. There is an account in one of the books of Moses in which Moses sent twelve spies to scope out the promised land

and its inhabitants to prepare the nation of Israel to enter it. When the spies returned, ten of them expressed their fear of the inhabitants, declaring that they could never defeat them. Two of the spies insisted the Israelites would still be victorious, but the people grumbled and took on the perspective of the ten who were afraid. (See Numbers 13:1–3, 26–33; 14:4.) As a result, the victory was delayed for forty years—almost two generations. The people lost out, largely because they allowed themselves to be influenced by the fearful mindset of others.

In contrast, when someone holds deep convictions, they can transfer those convictions to other people. For instance, they can rouse the fearful so that they will take bold and necessary action in the midst of a crisis. Winston Churchill, through his powerful speeches, stirred the English people to continue standing against Nazi Germany after the fall of France. In one of these speeches, he famously declared, "The Battle of France is over. I expect that the Battle of Britain is about to begin.... Let us therefore brace ourselves to our duties, and so bear ourselves that, if the British Empire and its Commonwealth last for a thousand years, men will still say, '*This* was their finest hour.'"[15] Churchill influenced the citizens of his nation to maintain courage and resilience under circumstances of extreme testing.

Thought: Someone who holds deep convictions can rouse the fearful so that they will take bold and necessary action in the midst of a crisis.

Reading: Numbers 13:1–3, 26–33; 14:4

15. Winston S. Churchill, ed., *Never Give In!: The Best of Winston Churchill's Speeches* (New York: Hyperion, 2003), 229.

—Day 84—

THE IMPACT OF INFLUENCE, PART 2

"When the wicked rise to power, people go into hiding; but when the wicked perish, the righteous thrive."

—Proverbs 28:28

Today, we continue to explore ways in which someone of influence can impact others in either a positive or negative way. The ethics of someone with influence can sway those who admire and/or follow them. This can occur through people either accepting the corporate values and policies that the individual encourages as a leader of a group or imitating (or accepting) their behavior. Many leaders feel they should experience no consequences when they betray the trust of their constituents—whether their employees, their families, or the public. Such attitudes and behaviors do not go unnoticed by followers, so that many people may begin to think, "He's a leader, and he did such and such and got away with it, so I can do it, too."

In contrast, an individual's strong convictions and commitment can be transferred to enough people that their personal convictions eventually become a positive movement. Their principles can initiate an irresistible process of reform. Martin Luther King Jr.'s vision gave him a passion that inspired and influenced "average" people—such as housewives, carpenters, masons, teachers, and religious leaders—to march in nonviolent protest against the refusal of certain states within the US to acknowledge and permit voting rights for Blacks. A number of them personally faced the resistance of policemen armed with clubs, dogs, water hoses, and tear gas. Why would anyone willingly risk being beaten with a billy club or choked by tear gas? What kind of man would influence people to actually do that? Someone with genuine commitment and conviction.

If you try to avoid an issue or a consequence, people won't follow you. But if you meet it squarely and remain constant in your convictions, others will join you.

A person of influence who lacks character can condemn those who follow them to an appalling fate, but the influence of someone who holds convictions can lead people to a positive destiny they might not otherwise have reached. Czech playwright and dissident Václav Havel, who had long decried the dehumanizing elements of communism, helped precipitate the nonviolent Velvet Revolution in Czechoslovakia in 1989 that effectively led to the end of communist rule there. Havel and other dissidents formed the Civic Forum to plan the dismantlement of communism in their country. Timothy Garton Ash, a historian who witnessed the forum, said, "It was extraordinary the degree to which everything ultimately revolved around this one man.... In almost all the forum's major decisions and statements, he was the final arbiter, the one person who could somehow balance the very different tendencies and interests in the movement."[16] Havel became the last president of Czechoslovakia and the first president of a new Czech Republic.

Thus, the impact of influence can be varied and pervasive. In our final devotions in this book, we will explore how you can use the influence that comes from success in an inspirational and honorable way to bring positive change in the world.

Thought: The influence of someone who holds convictions can lead people to a positive destiny they might not otherwise have reached.

Reading: Proverbs 28:1–12

16. Dan Bilefsky and Jane Perlez, "Vaclav Havel, Former Czech President, Dies at 75," December 18, 2011, http://www.nytimes.com/2011/12/19/world/europe/vaclav-havel-dissident-playwright-who-led-czechoslovakia-dead-at-75.html.

—Day 85—

TRANSFORMATION THROUGH INFLUENCE

"For the earth will be filled with the knowledge of the glory of the Lord as the waters cover the sea." —Habakkuk 2:14

One of my goals in writing about success and influence is to encourage you to be willing to become part of the answer to the challenges facing your community and nation. My desire is that you would go into the world and contribute to its transformation, duplicating in the lives of others what you have learned about how to discover inherent purpose and gifting and how to live according to the laws and principles of life. It is easy for us to criticize and complain about the state of the world. Let our days of complaining end so that we can become a solution to the problems we face, working to correct what is wrong.

Many nations in the world are struggling, and our world systems are in flux and in dire need of help. Across the globe, we have seen turbulent changes such as the following: Political confusion. Economic crisis. Ideological reinvention. Philosophical confusion. Moral manipulation. Values vacillation. Religious conflict. International terrorism. Failed states. The fall and disgrace of political, civic, and religious leaders. This is the kind of world we live in. We have to learn to adapt to these changes but not to adopt them.

When we consider the condition of the world and the many needs people have, we must remember that whatever we allow, we cannot criticize. Whatever we avoid, we cannot change. Whatever we permit, we are responsible for. If we don't become involved in addressing the needs around us, we have to keep quiet about them.

If you have been praying about the world situation, you must become part of the answer to your own prayer. You must go into the territory of *influence*.

Let us be people of initiative. To take initiative, we must study, think about, and discern the environment in which we live, discovering how to effectively apply the Creator's life-giving principles to it. God's number one passion is to manifest the influence of the kingdom of heaven and its culture on earth. Culture has to do with the setting in which something develops. To culture something means to grow something in a created environment.[17] God's plan is to create the environment of heaven on earth within which everything on earth is meant to grow. That is why the first word that the Creator used for Adam's environment was the word *Eden*: "*Now the* L*ORD* *God had planted a garden in the east, in Eden; and there he put the man he had formed*" (Genesis 2:8).

In my view, Eden is not a place. God "planted a garden." That doesn't mean God planted trees. The Hebrew word translated as "planted" can also mean "established." So, *planted* suggests something that is organized, and *garden* indicates structure or order.[18] God created an environment of order and then put human beings in it. He told them, in essence, "Multiply this all over the planet until the whole earth becomes like this spot, this environment." (See Genesis 1:27–28.)

Thought: If you have been praying about the world situation, you must become part of the answer to your own prayer.

Reading: Psalm 82:3–4

---

17. Merriam-Webster.com Dictionary, s.v. "culture," https://www.merriam-webster.com/dictionary/culture.
18. "5193. nata," Lexical Summary, Bible Hub, https://biblehub.com/hebrew/5193.htm.

—DAY 86—
SPEAK PEOPLE'S LANGUAGE

"I have become all things to all people so that by all possible means I might save some." —1 Corinthians 9:22

How do we go about making a difference in our environment? The first thing we must realize is that the world I described in yesterday's devotion cannot heal itself because the solution to the earth's problems is not found on earth. Those who have a solution from another place—God's kingdom, with its laws and principles—are valuable. That makes you valuable because you have reconnected to the other place. You have access to resources that many people on earth don't have.

In the midst of the world's upheaval, our goal, again, is influence—not domination or imposition. The culture of God's nature does not correspond with the destructive ideas that have developed from fallen human nature, and such ideas are dominating our nations today. It will take people of principle to bring about transformation and not merely become absorbed into the existing system.

Once more, you were born not just to make a living but to make a *difference*. If you get involved in making a difference, God will ensure that you make a living. Let your success be a vehicle by which you become an influence for good in the world around you.

As you live out the laws of success and grow in influence, there are various principles that will help you to effectively gain, exercise, and retain your influence. Today, we will look at the first of those principles: *Employ the language of your domain.*

We might also call this point "Speak people's language." Whatever the domain of your gifting, that's the place you're supposed to begin exercising a positive influence. And this means that you have to know the language of that particular environment and identify with its interests. Every field of endeavor or profession has its own language. You can't just go into any field and expect to succeed and be an influence in it if you aren't familiar with its language.

I keep studying the language of as many arenas as possible because I know I might find myself interacting with people in that environment. I use as my example Paul of Tarsus, who said, *"I have become all things to all people so that by all possible means I might save some."* He learned people's language and culture so he could relate to them, and they to him. If you read the teachings of Jesus, you might be amazed at how much He talked about birds, seeds, trees, fields, flowers, snakes, sheep, and so on. Why did He do this? Because the original audience to whom He was speaking lived in a farming culture. He spoke their language.

Thus, to help bring about change through positive influence, you must convey the message of God's kingdom, with its laws and principles of success, to those who are in your field or in whatever realm of life in which you are operating. However, you should communicate in a way that people can relate to and understand by using examples from their domain, as well as from everyday life and the experience of the wider world.

Thought: Let your success be a vehicle by which you become an influence for good in the world around you.

Reading: 1 Corinthians 9:19–23

—Day 87—

CONVINCE RATHER THAN OFFEND

"The fruit of the righteous is a tree of life, and the one who is wise saves lives." —Proverbs 11:30

In yesterday's devotion, we looked at a first principle of influence: employ the language of your domain, or speak people's language. A second essential principle is to use wisdom to *convince others rather than offend them*. In what way did God send Jesus into the earth to save the world? Wisely, through relatable influence. John, one of Jesus's closest disciples, wrote, *"The Word became flesh and made his dwelling among us. We have seen his glory, the glory of the one and only Son, who came from the Father, full of grace and truth"* (John 1:14). With Jesus, we are able to look upon the glory of God and not be afraid. God knew that in order to win people, He couldn't send someone whom people would be afraid of. His plan was, in effect, "I'm going to become just like them. They won't even recognize who I am until I've had an opportunity to show them My nature and teach them the laws and principles of My kingdom through influence."

One time, Jesus met a woman at a well and asked her for water. His approachable influence in that conversation was so effective that they ended up talking about deep matters that related to connecting with the Creator; this impacted not only the woman but her whole community as well. (See John 4:1–42.) When you interact with other people, no matter how right you may think you are, it needs to be with influence, not forcefulness; wisdom, not volume.

Jesus told His disciples, *"I send you out as sheep in the midst of wolves. Therefore be wise as serpents and harmless as doves"*

(Matthew 10:16 NKJV). There's that word *wise* again. I want you to understand the dynamics, the wisdom, of influence. Although you may experience "cultural clashes" with others as you live according to the Creator's principles and seek to share them, don't let those encounters cause you to respond in anger or fear toward other people. Use wisdom, and be patient. When you pursue your distinct purpose, attaining success and becoming a positive influence, you will fulfill your part in the purposes of God for the earth.

Again, we are called to convince, not offend. We won't influence people who are irritated to be around us! This applies to personal relationships, to business, to public service—every realm of life. It's not about how loud or direct you are. The goal is to persuade people, rather than offend them, by focusing on and communicating sound, life-giving principles.

We must take care in our interactions because once we offend someone, it's difficult to regain their trust. Solomon wrote, "*A brother offended is harder to win than a strong city, and contentions are like the bars of a castle*" (Proverbs 18:19 NKJV). The term "*strong city*" refers to a city with walls around it. The result of offense is contention. People who are offended will fight with you, argue with you, test you, and resist you. Instead, seek to build people up.

Thought: The goal is to persuade people, rather than offend them, by focusing on and communicating sound, life-giving principles.

Reading: John 4:1–26

—Day 88—

IMPACT RATHER THAN IMPOSE

"Let your conversation be always full of grace, seasoned with salt." —Colossians 4:6

One of the reasons I emphasized character in the previous section of this devotional is because character is the key to inspirational effectiveness. If we don't maintain good character, we jeopardize our influence. So, we must regularly ask ourselves, "Am I, in any way, violating the trust of those who have placed their faith in me? What impact am I having on those who are influenced or affected by my behavior?"

In an earlier devotion, we talked about the difference between laws and rules, and how rules are man-made traditions that restrict people rather than guide them and give them freedom. Thus, think about the ways in which you are interacting with people and carefully consider how you might be promoting mere tradition or rules rather than liberating laws and principles. Many people don't want to hear about tradition. They want to hear about principles that work, precepts that are valid. They want to know values and standards that are beneficial for them.

The goal of influence is impact rather than imposition. My wife and I traveled to a country where I had been invited to speak on leadership principles. In that country, it is illegal to talk about one's belief in Jesus. If you do, they will put you in jail. The people who had invited me asked me to speak to judges who served in the courts. (Those are the people who have the power to put you in jail!) They told me they wanted me to do a full-day seminar with these judges. So, I went into a hotel meeting room full of judges and talked to them about leadership.

After that, our hosts took us to a manufacturing plant where electronic products were made, and they said to me, "There are two thousand workers here. We want you to train them, as well as fifty or sixty managers, and then talk to the president of the company. You cannot mention God or Jesus." I said, "Give me the microphone." When I was finished, they invited me back. After every session, people bought all my books—books that, incidentally, had references to God and Jesus in them. We were sold out.

Now, they had told me I couldn't talk about Jesus, and I spoke for hours and never quoted a single passage from the Bible. I just spoke their language and emphasized the Creator's laws and principles. I talked to them about business and economics and science. I spoke about management and investment. I spoke about leadership, and the sessions were powerful. They kept saying to me, "Where did you learn this?" or "This is amazing information you have." In reply, I would say something like, "I had a young Rabbi as a mentor."

After I returned home, I started receiving emails from people who had heard my talks and bought my books and who had connected with God and with Jesus. I didn't impose my beliefs on them. My beliefs came out in my principles, and then the people made their own decision about them. That is influence without imposition or domination.

Thought: Consider how you might be promoting mere tradition or rules rather than liberating laws and principles.

Reading: Colossians 4:5–6

—Day 89—

MAKE FRIENDS, NOT "CONVERTS"

"Greater love has no one than this: to lay down one's life for one's friends." —John 15:13

As a person of influence, when you talk with other people, listen to their reasons for thinking and acting in the way that they do. Every human being on earth has a reason why they believe what they believe. If you ignore their reason, they will not listen to you, and they may even reject you. If you want to communicate the laws of creation, and someone says, "I'm an atheist," don't ignore that. There's a reason why they don't believe in God and that they believe what they believe. You can ask them, "Why are you an atheist?" and "What's the reason you came to this conclusion?"

Their answer may blow your mind. We have no idea what some people have been through. I talked with one man who, when he was a boy, was told by his mother that God loved both of them. Then, when he was only seven, his mother was raped and killed in front of him. The man said, "I told God, 'Go to he--.' There's no God. God didn't save my mother."

After I heard this, I said, "I see why you don't believe in God. I understand." All of a sudden, he liked me, and we became friends. We maintained a friendship, and, two years later, he reconnected with God and Jesus.

Jesus first made a friend of every person He influenced. Our goal should be the same. You can best serve someone's interests in life by being their friend. Solomon wrote, *"Faithful are the wounds of a friend, but the kisses of an enemy are deceitful"* (Proverbs 27:6 NKJV). In other words, once you are someone's friend, if you correct them, they will thank you for it. If you're my friend, I will listen to you. If you're my friend, you will gain my confidence. I will open up to you; again, I will confide in you and tell you my reasons for doing what I do.

You make friends with people when you become interested in what they are interested in. I previously mentioned how Jesus met a woman at a well and asked her for some water. He knew that this woman had had five husbands and was hurting, but He didn't bring up any of that until after they had begun to talk and she was ready to hear what He had to say.

We need to be committed to people because it may take years for them to open up to us and respond to what we have to say. Most people are just looking for a friend. You don't attack people whom you want to help. You love them. Jesus said, "*My command is this: Love each other as I have loved you. Greater love has no one than this: to lay down one's life for one's friends*" (John 15:12–13). We need to work on laying down our life for people.

Thought: In what ways are you being a friend to those whom you are influencing or would like to influence for good?

Reading: John 15:9–17

—DAY 90—

FULFILLING YOUR PURPOSE

"Being confident of this, that he who began a good work in you will carry it on to completion until the day of Christ Jesus."
—Philippians 1:6

It's important for you to truly understand that your success is personal. It comes from accomplishing the purpose that you, as an individual, were put on this earth to fulfill. It comes from completing the assignment for which you were born. As we have seen, the journey of success begins when you discover and activate your inherent gift. Remember that you came to earth because you are "finished"—you arrived with everything you need to fulfill your purpose and be successful. Once you know your gift, your ability to succeed in life is a result of the decisions you make to manifest what is inside you. Keep in mind that success is not a pursuit but a result. You never have to worry about being successful—if you serve your gift to the world, you will succeed!

We have also seen that you can carry out your purpose and assignment only by following the laws and principles established in creation. These laws and principles are among the greatest discoveries you can make in life. Once you understand these laws, they're not difficult to put into practice. A person who knows and follows laws and principles will always be successful. Thus, the key to living effectively on this earth is a knowledge of laws, an understanding of laws, a submission to laws, and an application of laws. When you obey laws, they will protect you. They will preserve you. They will sustain you. In the end, they will promote you. They will lead to your success and influence in the world.

Remember also that a fruit seed is successful only when it becomes a *fruit-bearing* tree. If such a seed becomes a tree alone, it is not yet successful. That tree must bear fruit, and the fruit must have seed within it as well. In other words, if you do only some of what you were meant to do in life, you haven't yet attained success. You have more of your assignment to fulfill. Thus, throughout your journey of success, endeavor to complete your purpose so that you will be able to say, as Paul of Tarsus did near the end of his life, *"I have fought the good fight, I have finished the race, I have kept the faith"* (2 Timothy 4:7). In essence, Paul was saying, "There's nothing left for me to accomplish. I have done everything that I was sent here to do."

This brings us back to the top five questions in life:

1. "Who am I?"
2. "Where am I from?"
3. "Why am I here?"
4. "What am I able to do?"
5. "Where am I going?"

I hope that you are now closer to answering these questions for yourself. My purpose has been to equip you with the knowledge and practical principles necessary to experience personal development for success and influence. Put into practice what you have learned throughout this devotional. Make the choice to become all that you were meant to be.

Thought: Your ability to succeed in life is a result of the decisions you make to manifest what is inside you.

Reading: 2 Timothy 4:6–8

ABOUT THE AUTHOR

Myles Munroe (1954–2014) was an international motivational speaker, best-selling author, educator, leadership mentor, and consultant for government and business. Traveling extensively throughout the world, Dr. Munroe addressed critical issues affecting the full range of human, social, and spiritual development. He was a popular author of more than forty books, including *The Spirit of Leadership, Becoming a Leader, The Principles and Power of Vision, The Power of Character in Leadership,* and the devotionals *A Leader of Purpose and Power, Vision with Purpose and Power, Prayer with Purpose and Power, A Woman of Purpose and Power,* and *A Man of Purpose and Power.*

Dr. Munroe was the founder and president of Bahamas Faith Ministries International (BFMI), a multidimensional organization headquartered in Nassau, Bahamas. He was the chief executive officer and chairman of the board of the International Third World Leaders Association and president of the International Leadership Training Institute.

Dr. Munroe earned B.A. and M.A. degrees from Oral Roberts University and the University of Tulsa and was awarded a number of honorary doctoral degrees. The parents of two adult children, Charisa and Chairo (Myles Jr.), Dr. Munroe and his wife, Ruth, traveled as a team and were involved in teaching seminars together. Both were leaders who ministered with sensitive hearts and international vision. In November 2014, they were tragically killed in an airplane crash en route to an annual leadership conference sponsored by Bahamas Faith Ministries International. A statement from Dr. Munroe in his book *The Power of Character in Leadership* summarizes his own legacy: "Remember that character ensures the longevity of leadership, and men and women of principle will leave important legacies and be remembered by future generations."